CHAKRAS

CHAKRAS

—

Balance your
vital energies

JULIAN FLANDERS

SIRIUS

SIRIUS

This edition published in 2020 by Sirius Publishing, a division of
Arcturus Publishing Limited,
26/27 Bickels Yard, 151–153 Bermondsey Street,
London SE1 3HA

Copyright © Arcturus Holdings Limited

ISBN: 978-1-83857-635-6
AD007322UK

Printed in China

Contents

Introduction
What are chakras?

The word chakra is derived from the Sanskrit word *cakra*, meaning 'wheel' or 'circle'. Inside our bodies, we have a number of whirling, vortex-like centres of natural energy that, taken together, form a channel for the integration of mind, body and spirit. This invisible energy, often called *prana*, is our life force and, when in balance, keeps us vibrant, healthy and alive.

It is important to understand that chakras have no physicality, but, corresponding to nerve centres in the body, they act like water currents directing energy up and down the body and around the major organs. There are seven main chakras, which start at the base of the spine and go up to the crown of the head. They sit in the subtle body (see pages 19-21) at points where matter and consciousness meet, providing us with a connecting channel between our minds and our bodies, our physical being and our spiritual selves, the past, the present and the future. In this way, the chakras can have an influence on both our physical and our emotional lives.

In her book *Wheels of Life*, Anodea Judith suggests that 'chakras are organising centres for the reception, assimilation and transmission of life energies'. Although the human body is an amazing machine, performing incredible feats every day, from sending signals rocketing through the brain at high speed to distributing oxygen over 1,000 miles (1,600 kilometres) of airways, it can do nothing without energy. Judith sees the chakras as 'the wheels of life that carry [us] through trials, tribulations and transformations'.

Given the way chakras can be said to govern our lives, it is essential that they remain open, aligned and fluid. Because mind and body are completely interrelated, one blocked chakra is likely to affect another. These blockages can be: physical, such as a tumour, a cyst, a stomach ache or a sore throat; emotional, perhaps in the form of anxiety or depression; psychological, spiritual, karmic or energetic. It will also depend on which chakra is blocked. For example, if your third chakra is affected, then you might experience a lack of confidence or self-esteem, indigestion, shame or an allergic reaction. If your fifth chakra is blocked then you might find it difficult to communicate ideas, suffer from a lack of creativity, or from problems with your neck or shoulders.

In any spiritual practice, awareness is the first step towards healing. For some, this means stepping out of the dark into the light; for others, it means realising that you have put weight on and that you must do something about it. The aim of this book is to make you aware of your chakras and how they can have a positive effect on your life. There are chapters on each of the chakras, how to open and balance them through meditation and yoga, how to feed them, and how to heal them, should they become blocked.

Part One

THE CHAKRAS

The history of chakras

The concept of chakras originally came from ancient India. The first references are found in the *Vedas* (which literally means 'knowledge') and the *Upanishads* (see page 12). Now regarded as some of the most sacred scripts of Hinduism, these are collections of religious texts, poems, prayers, songs and stories. They include material that had been transmitted orally over many generations among the local population of north-western India, including the Sanskrit-speaking Aryans from the Indus valley. As the dominant language of the region, these texts were written in the Aryan language.

Although the authorship of the texts is unclear, the worldview, social attitudes and spiritual preoccupations recorded tend to reflect those of the Brahmans, the priestly class, of ancient India. They also hint at the

beginnings of the caste system in the region at the top of which sat the Brahmans, above the Kshatriyas (warriors), the Vaishyas (landowners and merchants) and the Shudras (labourers). It seems logical, even from this distance, that those that controlled the writing and distribution of texts such as these would be the dominant caste in such a primitive society.

However, the word *cakra* used in these ancient texts did not refer to psychic energy centres, but rather to a circle, as in a seasonal cycle or the wheel of time. It was also used in a political sense, referring to the wheel of a chariot, symbolic of political power and influence. The use of the term to indicate energy vortices first appeared much later, in medieval Hindu and Buddhist texts.

COMMUNICATING WITH THE GODS

At that time (the *Vedas* were written between 1500 and 1200 BCE), India was an agricultural society, dependent on water and the natural cycle of the seasons. The people believed in many gods and spirits, often relating to natural forces, such as storms, wind and fire, and included those living in animals, trees, rivers and mountains. Some of the gods were good and others bad, but the most revered were those chosen by the Vedic priests. The myths surrounding the gods, such as Indra, the god of storms and of war, and Agni, the god of fire and soma, who was the personification of the soma plant – whose holy

Sandstone relief of the tantric meditation deity, the goddess Tara, at a 12th century Jain temple in Rajasthan, India.

juice was intoxicating to both gods and men – provided the link between humans and the gods.

In order to communicate with the gods to maintain the balance of the cosmos, the priests would conduct rituals and sacrifices. To perform these sacred ceremonies, the priests had to reach a state of bliss. They did this through meditation in which they held poses that would open their bodies and minds to the deities; it is claimed that these poses are the earliest examples of yoga. The priests hoped that in return for these rituals and sacrifices, the gods would offer protection from the bad spirits.

REJECTION OF THE VEDIC TRADITION

However, as nature is not dependent on rituals, when things went wrong and rain washed out the crops or drought occurred, people would question the priests' intentions. Some sense of the rejection of priestly ideas and religious practices appeared in new texts published as the *Upanishads* (*c.* 900 BCE). Somewhere around the beginning of the 7th century BCE, a new culture of world-renunciation began, shifting the focus of religious life away from rights and sacrifices that were rejected as they did not work. Although adherents to this new system retained certain elements of previous practice, notably meditation and yoga, their spiritual quests for truth became internal rather than external. The priests condemned these new ideas as 'heretical', but over time religion in the Vedic tradition was rejected and replaced by new movements, such as Charvaka, Jainism and Buddhism, that originated around this time.

THE CLASSIC CHAKRA SYSTEMS

Most historians agree that Hinduism, which developed between 500 BCE and 300 CE, is where the concepts of chakras as part of ancient meditation practices, known as *Tantra* (see pages 15-18), originated. A theory developed suggesting that human life had two parallel dimensions, one physical (the mass of the human body) and the other non-physical (energy or the subtle body), which interacted with each other. The subtle body (see pages 19-21) consisted of *nadi* (energy channels) which circulated around the body. The focal points at which this interaction took place were known as *chakras*. The number of chakras believed to be present in a human body varied widely, but the main ones, normally believed to be between four and seven, were arranged along the spinal cord. Tantric traditions developed, seeking to awaken the chakras and energise them through meditation and breathing techniques. The chakras, though not

A young priest sits in meditation under a banyan tree – such practices are used to achieve a state of bliss and communion with the gods.

physical in form, were mapped and matched to a person's psychological state, sounds, deities, colours and other motifs.

These traditions varied widely within Hinduism and there were similar ideas in other cultures too, notably Chinese medicine, Tibetan Buddhism, Jewish Kabbalah, Malayan and Indonesian metaphysical theory, among others. They all shared the concept of a 'life energy' and the existence of psycho-spiritual 'organs' or faculties, the activation of which make a person complete. Traditional Chinese Medicine relied on a similar model of the human body as an energy system; Tantric Buddhism emphasised 'organic harmony', often achieved through yoga; the Kabbalah believed the key to spirituality was self-awareness, achieved by connecting the physical body and its etheric counterpart; while the Silat tradition of the Malay Archipelago believed that defensive and offensive energy rotates through the body along diagonal lines.

Tantra

Tantra is a word originally used to denote early esoteric traditions of Hindu and Buddhist adherents, and it is the source of the concept of chakras. Many of these traditions centred around deities, such as Vishnu,

An illustration depicting the union of Shiva and Shakti energy through the chakras.

the 'Supreme Being', Shiva and Shakti. Believers held that all realities were the product of the relationship between Shakti, the mother of the universe, and Shiva, the energy of all existence. She the life-giver; he formless until given life. Early tantric texts often took the form of conversations between the two deities, which revealed how much they depended on one another. Arthur Avalon explains the relationship in his book *The Serpent Power* (see page 28): 'There is no power-holder without power. No power without power-holder. Power is Shakti, the Great Mother of the universe. There is no Shiva without Shakti, or Shakti without Shiva.'

Shiva and Shakti are often depicted in statues and images in a constant embrace, creating the universe through their love, much as life is created by a woman using the man's seed. The intention of their union was also to achieve a state of bliss. But as well as creating life, the two are seen as forming a bridge between the earthly (Shakti) and the divine (Shiva), between the body and the spirit, between the Earth and heaven. This concept of balance is further reflected in the idea that the energy passing through the chakras in our bodies flows both upwards and downwards; it moves down to feed the body and soul, and up towards creativity and freedom. Tantric traditions also embraced the elements: earth, fire, air, water and space (ether), which are regarded as the raw materials of existence. It is because of this that each chakra is associated with one of the elements.

One of the earliest tantric belief systems was Shaivism. First recorded in the Kashmir Valley from about 600 BCE, it is one of the earliest sources of postural asana yoga practices. This was followed by hatha yoga, which can be traced back to around 1100 BCE. Since then, tantric traditions have developed in many Eastern religions, from Jainism and Shinto to Daoism and Tibetan Bön, examples of which are often seen in temple building, artworks and other imagery across Southeast Asia.

The use of the word tantra to refer to all esoteric practice and ritual is an invention from colonial-era Europe. The term, which means 'loom', was used as a metaphor for weaving separate threads into one whole entity, creating the fabric of existence, linking mind and body, man and woman, the physical and the spiritual.

Illustration from a 19th century yoga manuscript in the Braja-bhasa language depicting the chakras and energetic correspondences of the body.

In the early years of the 20th century, a yogi and occultist called Pierre Bernard began introducing and monetising the philosophy and practices of tantra to his native America. He did raise its profile, but a series of scandals centring around his schools for teaching what he called 'mystical sex techniques' saw him discredited and created a misleading impression of its connection to sex, an impression that still survives today. Modern tantric practices do contain a sexual element, normally associated with the goddess Kundalini, as one way of achieving bliss, though this can equally be obtained through celibacy. Tantric practices, including yoga, meditation and caring for your chakras, are other ways to achieve liberation. In tantra, the body is a temple and should be kept purified and healthy, through yoga, breathing techniques and a healthy diet – things that will help ensure sexual pleasure.

Of course, tantra is more than that. According to Sanskrit scholar and tantric teacher Christopher Wallis, 'Tantra is fundamentally a world-embracing rather than world-denying [philosophy]. It focuses on the imminent rather than the transcendent, integrating with everyday life rather than renouncing it.' For him, the tantric view is that the world and everything in it is an expression of the divine and that seeking a deeper awareness of it all, through tantra, leads to realisation.

The subtle body

Chakras do not exist physically in the body, rather they exist in something called the subtle body, which is comprised of a number of vibrating energy fields that surround every living thing, from a cell to a plant to a human being. Together these bands of energy make up the auric field.

Experts argue about the number of fields present around a human body (some say six, some seven and others twelve), but they do agree that these fields overlay our physical selves and provide a space for interaction between mind and body. They regulate all our physical and spiritual functions in correspondence with various parts of the subtle body.

A corona of light, or halo, around Jesus Christ and his disciples is believed by some to depict the subtle body and its external manifestation in the aura.

The physical body generates energy that vibrates slowly, in this way it appears to our physical eyes to be solid. As you move out from the physical body to the invisible layers of the auric field, which includes the etheric body, the emotional body, the mental body, the astral body, the etheric template body, the celestial body and the causal body (sometimes referred to as the ketheric template), each field vibrates slightly faster than the previous one. Each of these layers connect to the physical body via energy points – the chakras – which direct energy into the physical body via the *nadis* and the meridian system.

The term 'subtle body' is used in a number of esoteric teachings including Hinduism, Buddhism and Jainism, and there are a number of different theories about the importance of these auric layers. Some define the subtle body as that part of our being or consciousness that leaves our body at the time of physical death. Others describe it as the part of the body that perceives sensation, for example, where amputees feel 'pain' or 'itching' in their missing limbs. Another theory is that it includes the subtle sense organs (the aspect of our five sense organs with which we are able to perceive the subtle realm) and the subtle motor organs (all activity in our physical motor organs is first initiated in our subtle motor organs).

Perhaps the most outlandish theory came from the scientist Rupert Sheldrake in the early 1980s. He suggested that a 'morphogenetic' layer was also present in the auric field. In biology, a morphogenic field is a group of cells that leads to specific tissues or organs, and that because only living organisms that belong to a certain group can tune in to a particular morphic resonance. In this way, a dog, for example, would not develop the characteristics of a plant and so on.

Sheldrake took the idea further, suggesting that the morphogenic field might actually sit alongside DNA in explaining how certain behaviours, characteristics and emotions are carried down through a family, particularly when separated by time and space. His theory was that past life memories could pass from lifetime to lifetime through a soul's morphic energy field. These memories would be non-local nor anchored in the brain or in a particular life. This could explain, for example, how a grandad's talent as a fine artist was carried on to his grandson.

Taken together, the layers of the auric field make up what is more popularly known as the aura.

The aura

The aura is the external manifestation of the subtle body, an 'energy skin' that protects the energy of the human body much as physical skin protects the inner organs. It surrounds the body like an egg-shaped cocoon. This phenomenon has been recognised by many cultures and religions throughout history, including the coronas of light around Jesus and his disciples in Christian iconography, the Kabbalist tradition of astral light, and in the teachings of the Vedic scriptures.

A human's aura is created by the action of the life-force energy, *prana*, within the body. It resonates through the chakras and both the physical and subtle anatomy. The auric field is similar to an electromagnetic field emanating from an electrical device. It can be perceived as colour, brightness, shape or density. Some can hear it, as sound or vibration, and others can feel the aura's energy, through heartbeat or body temperature.

Someone's auric colour reflects their current energy status, often appearing in multiple layers of various rainbow colours. Many things can affect the shade of each layer of colour, from simple things like mood to more major issues such as spiritual development. It can change from minute to minute or remain a steady shade and intensity for longer periods of time.

If you have ever met a professional sportsman or woman you might have noticed the power and strength emanating from them, indicating an aura at its peak of health. If someone is healthy, self-confident, calm and grounded, their aura will be clean and brightly-coloured; they will emanate strong vibrations, strong tones and will have a full, smoothly shaped boundary. In contrast, the aura of someone who is ill, depressed or unsure of him or herself, would be thinner and dull-coloured. Its vibrations would be slow and even erratic and it might have a break or tear in the boundary.

Because the aura has been such a universally accepted phenomenon for so long, there has been a considerable amount of scientific investigation into its mysteries, particularly since the 1880s. An early theory, posited by Jan Baptist van Helmond, suggested it acted like a fluid. This was further developed by Franz Mesmer, of 'mesmerism'

A coloured etching depicting a scene in which a number of patients in Paris receive Mesmer's animal magnetism therapy.

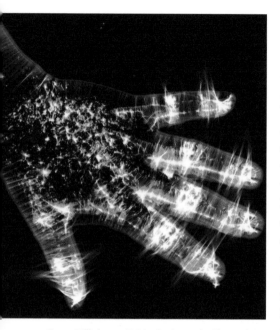

Baron Wilhelm von Reichenbach was the first to relate the human energy field to different colours, which Kirlian photography later made visible to the eye.

fame, who suggested that both animate and inanimate objects were charged with a magnetic fluid by which material bodies could exert influence over each other. Baron Wilhelm von Reichenbach was the first to relate the human energy field to different colours. He agreed that the aura could carry a charge and described the field on the left-hand side of the body as a negative pole and the right as positive. This is an idea mirrored in Chinese medicine.

A particular area of interest has also been how to 'see' auras, since clairvoyance, though effective and enormously popular in the Victorian era, was not evidence enough for many sceptics. In 1911, Dr Walter Kilner conducted an experiment that first established the connection between the auric energy field and the human body. Using specially designed goggles, he was able to see a patient's aura and detect a shift in the condition of it in reaction to their state of mind and their health. He proposed its use in medical diagnosis and prognosis.

In the 1930s, research began to focus on what were then called 'bio-currents' emanating from the human body. Russian scientists were able to measure energy fields, discovering that living organisms emanate vibrations at a frequency between 300 and 2,000 nanometres. Another development occurred in Russia when scientists Semyon and Valentina Kirlian developed a process that involved directing a high-frequency electrical field at someone and then taking photographs. The photos revealed the person's pattern of luminescence – their auric energy field. Practitioners today still use Kirlian photography to reveal patients' emotional and mental states and even to diagnose illnesses and other problems.

In 1988, computer technology enabled Dr Valerie Hunt to record electrical signals emanating from the human body during Rolfing (a type of alternative healing bodywork) sessions with her patients. The wave-patterns were then analysed and revealed that the energy fields did actually consist of different coloured bands, which in all cases correlated with the colours associated with the chakras. The slowest, measured in hertz, being blue, then green, yellow, orange, red, violet and white. Dr Hunt took things a little further, inviting a psychic to use intuitive perception to work out the aura of the same patients. In all cases, the renderings produced were the same as those demonstrated by the technology.

Part Two

THE
SEVEN-CHAKRA
SYSTEM

A brief guide

Although they are all originally from the same tantric tradition, there have been five-chakra, six-chakra, seven-, nine-, ten-, twelve-, twenty-one and more chakra systems taught through history. There are major chakras, usually corresponding to parts of the spine, and a multitude of lesser chakras, for example, in your hands, feet, joints and back. But it is the Shakta seven-chakra system that is now commonly accepted in the West. The history of this system goes back to a tenth century text, the *Kubjika-mata-tantra*, which taught a system incorporating six major chakras arranged along the axial channel of the human body, with a seventh point at the top, not then regarded as a chakra.

The popularity of this system was boosted in the early years of the 20th century through the publication of a book called *The Serpent Power*, written by the British orientalist Sir John Woodroffe (also known as Arthur Avalon) in 1918. This was a translation of the *Sat-cakra-nirupana*, a Sanskrit text written in 1577 by Purnananda Yati. This was followed in 1927 by an even more remarkable book, *The Chakras*, by Charles Webster Leadbeater, a prominent clairvoyant and theosophist, in which the author described each of the by-then seven chakras in exquisite detail, including its placement on the body, size, shape, colours and even vibratory pulsations. He also illustrated each 'circle', painting them, as he claims, from detailed accounts of individuals who were able to see the chakras using clairvoyant powers.

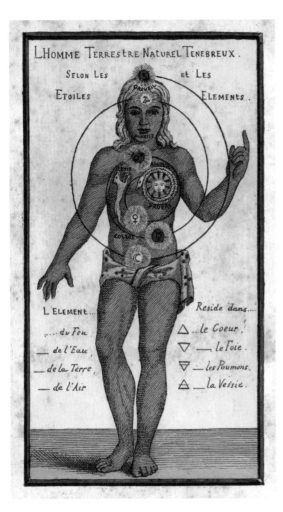

The chakras according to Johann Georg Gichtel, showing the four elements and where they reside in the body.

Purist critics are often dubious about the provenance of these works, claiming that the chakra concept today bears little resemblance to that originally envisaged in the *Vedas* and *Upanishads* and point out that many of its elements are incorrect and some are even untrue. However, while the seven-chakra system is only one of many models and has many

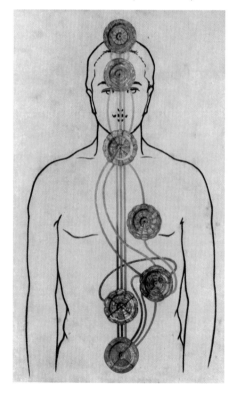

elements that have been added during recent years, meaning that it bears little resemblance to the ancient practices on which it is based, this is the system that has been adopted in the West and more widely across the world. Perhaps even more persuasive is the fact that present-day Indian gurus also use this theory within their system of philosophy and teachings.

The positioning of the seven chakras according to Charles Webster Leadbeater.

According to Christopher Wallis, however, there are certain elements of current Western teaching about chakras that do come from original sources. Chakras are visualised as lotus flowers with a different number of petals in each one. The mystical sounds of the Sanskrit alphabet are associated with the lotus petals of each of the chakras in the system. This is helpful in the meditation used to open each chakra, providing a template for *nyasa* ('placing') by giving you a specific mantric syllable to access a specific chakra by silently, or otherwise, intoning its sound.

Each chakra is also associated with a specific element (earth, water, fire, wind and space), its relevant colour, and a specific Hindu deity or deities. The seven chakras are described as being aligned in an ascending column along the major nerve ganglia from the base of the spine to the top of the head. In modern practice, each chakra is associated with a certain colour. Chakras are associated with multiple physiological functions, an aspect of consciousness, a classical element, and other distinguishing characteristics. These are all included in the chapters on each chakra that follow later on in the book in order to give you as complete a picture as possible of each chakra.

Below are brief descriptions of the seven chakras and their main characteristics. Before reading, it is important to remember that chakras are not 'things'. As Lar Short, co-author of *The Body of Light*, a seminal book on the inner workings of all spiritual traditions says, 'You cannot cut open a yogi and find chakras, any more than you can dissect an opera singer and find librettos and songs.' But they do exist within the subtle body, exhibiting a strong influence on such things as body shape, health, well-being and wholeness.

Muladhara (see page 36)

The root chakra, also known as the base chakra, is located at the base of the spine. It helps to keep the energy of the body grounded and connected with earthly energies. Helps movement, survival and self-esteem.

Svadhisthana (see page 48)

The sacral chakra is located in the lower abdomen, between the navel and the genitals; this chakra is associated with your kidneys, bladder, circulatory system and your reproductive organs and glands. It is concerned with emotion and represents desire, pleasure, sexuality, procreation and creativity.

Manipura (see page 60)

The solar plexus chakra seeks to achieve balance in self-esteem issues and intuitive skills. This chakra is associated with your digestive system, muscles, pancreas and adrenal glands. Your sensitivity, ambition and ability to achieve are stored here. It can be seen as the seat of your emotional life and is associated with feelings of personal power, laughter, joy and anger.

Anahata (see page 70)

The heart chakra is the centre of love, harmony, compassion and peace. Many call it the 'house of the soul'. It is important to keep this chakra in balance so that we can remain in the right emotional state. Heartbreak or emotional abuse can affect not only the heart, but also your lungs, arms, hands and the thymus gland, which produces T cells to boost the immune system.

Vishuddha (see page 84)

The throat chakra is symbolised by the colour of the sky, either light blue or turquoise. The name, translated from the original Sanskrit, means 'purification' or 'cleansing'. It affects our ability to communicate. In balance, it helps inspire calmness, assisting us with right speech, honesty and good decision-making. However, not being able to express ourselves properly can lead to anxiety, a cold, a sore throat or an ear infection.

Ajna (see page 96)

Known as the third eye chakra, this is located in the centre of the head, slightly above the eyes and between the eyebrows. This is the seat of wisdom and insight, and helps keep things in perspective. Its colour is a deep, rich indigo and it is said to be the link between the higher and the lower self. This chakra is used to question the spiritual nature of our life. It is the chakra of question, perception and knowing. It is concerned with inner vision, intuition and wisdom. It also holds your dreams for this life and recollections of other lifetimes.

Sahasrara (see page 108)

This chakra sits on the top of the head. It is the highest form of chakra, which opens up spiritual communication between the body and the universe, the finite and the infinite. It is said to be the chakra of divine purpose and personal destiny. It is concerned with information, understanding, acceptance and bliss. It is the receiver and giver of energy. Some traditions associate it with the colour white, others with violet. It is often represented by a thousand-petalled lotus flower.

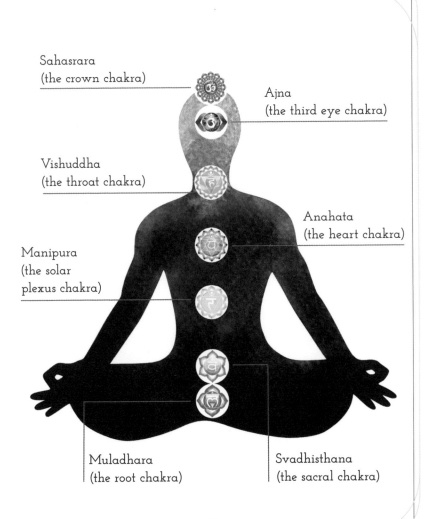

Sahasrara
(the crown chakra)

Ajna
(the third eye chakra)

Vishuddha
(the throat chakra)

Anahata
(the heart chakra)

Manipura
(the solar
plexus chakra)

Muladhara
(the root chakra)

Svadhisthana
(the sacral chakra)

The First Chakra
MULADHARA

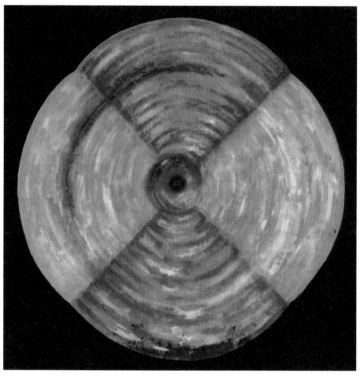

COMMON NAME
The root chakra

LOCATION
The perineum, at
the base of the spine
between the anus and
the genitals

ELEMENT
Earth

COLOUR
Red

SENSE
Smell

BIJA (SEED) MANTRA
Lam, Om

YANTRA SYMBOL
A four-petalled lotus
with a square inside
and an inverted triangle
inside that

ASSOCIATED DEITIES
Brahma, Ganesha,
Dakini

GEMS AND STONES
Ruby, bloodstone, garnet

Everyone is able to see the beauty of the leaves and flowers of a plant, but few stand in admiration of the roots that lie hidden in the earth below. However, the roots are essential for the survival of any land plant: they anchor it in its place, they absorb water and nutrients from the soil, and they store food. Through this system the plant gains the strength and the power to penetrate the soil, growing upwards towards the sun to produce flowers, fruit and seeds.

The Muladhara – or root chakra – plays a similar role for the human being. Located at the base of the spine, in the place sometimes known as the pelvic floor, this chakra is responsible for your sense of safety and security. As the focal point of our connection to the earth, situated at the top of our legs and the bottom of our bodies, this is the building block on which our existence is based.

This chakra relates to the element earth and provides the grounding you need in your life; this covers basic needs such as food, water and shelter as well as safety, health, material and emotional needs.

The process starts just after conception; at the centre of the soon-to-be foetus is a ball of energy, the *prana* or 'life force', around which the physical body then begins to form.

After birth, the right loving care will mean that the child feels secure in the world, trusting that his or her needs will be met. If that care is not given, or is inconsistent then it might manifest itself as chakra blockages in later life.

Electrical connections

With stable foundations and our feet firmly planted, we are connected to the earth through gravity. Being grounded in this way gives us the reassurance we need to find our way in the world. With a stable base, we are able to concentrate our energies in a positive way, without fear. Contact with the earth also provides us with energy, as we move through our lives. The Earth is surrounded with an electrostatic field caused by geophysical phenomena, such as ionization, ultraviolet radiation from the sun, convection, precipitation and so on. This resonates with micromotions in the body, such as our heartbeat and the movement of bodily fluids, which is helped by the energy that flows up from the earth, though our bodies, and back down through our legs and feet.

Of course, energy is also generated through exercise, and this is an essential tool in balancing the first chakra. So move, walk, run, jump, swim, play football, get a dog, whatever takes your fancy. Do it regularly, make it part of your daily routine. The more exercise you do, the more energy you will generate.

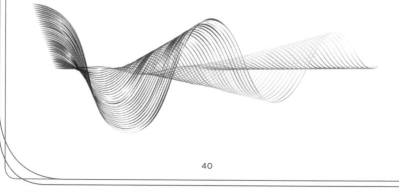

Being grounded helps us feel complete, balanced and stable both bodily and in the mind. As Muladhara is the first of the bodily chakras, keeping it in balance also creates a solid foundation for the chakras that sit above it.

Body and mind

The body and the mind are in constant interaction during our lives. It is a complex relationship. The Muladhara chakra is the seat of the unconscious. It is here that we hold our flight-or-fight response. It is here that we store or deepest, darkest memories, our hurts, heartbreaks and disappointments. When this chakra becomes active, it can reveal aspects of our characters that we do not necessarily like, such as destructive rage, deep-seated anger or excessive desires. We can also find that we are suffering from an imbalance in the root chakra, which may be mental, such as anxiety or nightmares, or physical, which may manifest itself as a problem in the colon, with the bladder, with elimination, or with pains in the lower back, legs, or feet. This begs the question as to whether it is better to allow the unconscious to remain buried rather than stir it up and suffer, again.

The answer is not hard to find. It is only by facing the ills of the past can we let go of our fear in the present. Only when we have faced our weaknesses, regrets and bad decisions can we move forward with purpose. We must learn that we are not only responsible for what we do, but also for what we do not do.

Although it hides our secrets, the Muladhara chakra is also the mother who nourishes and raises us. It is also the seat of our dormant wisdom, the stronghold of our emotional strength and other hidden abilities. If you face up to your regrets and the painful feelings in your consciousness, they are brought to the surface where they can be healed. Along with the bad memories come good ones, as we remember how we overcame adversity, how much we loved those we have lost, how we have felt joy, harmony and freedom. You can learn from your mistakes through reflection, become conscious of the right thing to do and find the strength to move forward with the right intentions. In this way, we can remove the yolk of past mistakes and clear our path into the future. Revisiting past disappointments can be a positive process, as it can be a transition, a step in our development.

The yantra and associated deities

Yantras are geometric devices used to facilitate meditation. The use of these images comes from the Tantric traditions of Indian religions and were made popular in the West by the psychologist Carl Jung (1875–1961) who found that drawing and colouring them helped him overcome rational thought and access his unconscious. Each of the chakras has a yantra associated with it, which typically includes geometric shapes, deities and other symbols. As well as meditation, yantras can be used for protection, good fortune and healing.

The Muladhara yantra, which is red in colour, has four lotus petals, inside which is a square. Both are representations of the four points of

the compass and four aspects of consciousness: mind, intellect, consciousness and ego.
Inside the square are four more symbols:
an image of the seed sound (lam – see
below), which is said to contain the essence
of the chakra; an elephant with seven trunks;
a downward-pointing triangle inside which

is a crescent moon and a phallus with a snake coiled around it. The
elephant, associated with the elephant-headed god Ganesha, represents
strength, its seven trunks indicating the power needed to support all
seven major chakras. The triangle represents Shakti (female) energy,
while the phallus, or Shiva lingam, represents male energy. Wrapped
around this is a coiled snake; this represents Kundalini (an energy
and goddess associated with higher consciousness) which is rooted
in the Muladhara chakra. Other deities associated with the first
chakra are Brahma, the creator of the universe, and his consort,
the goddess Dakini.

The bija (seed) mantra

Mantras have been used as an aid to mediation for thousands
of years. They can be chanted out loud or silently in order to
find an inward focus. When sounded out loud, the sound
should be extended so that each repetition runs into
the next, creating a drone sound. The most
famous, *om*, is the symbol of the Absolute

and represents the merging of our physical and spiritual bodies. It is sometimes written as 'aum' because you should begin with the ahh sound in the back of your throat, bringing the sound forward in your mouth to 'ooo' and 'mmm' with your lips closed. This chant can be used to awaken any or all of your chakras, but each chakra has its own seed mantra too. The seed mantra for the Muladhara chakra is *lam* (pronounced 'larm'), the sound of spiritual awakening. It releases tensions, removes blockages and activates its energy. And so the process of awakening the dormant powers within us and raising them into consciousness begins.

Meditation

Meditation is a good way of awakening your chakras. This will help you in many ways, enabling you to recognise when they are in balance as well as identifying any imbalance or blockages as they occur. The following meditations, one sitting inside and one standing outside, will start the process of awareness for the first chakra. Should you identify a problem, move on to the yoga poses (*asanas*) for help in healing and rebalancing (see pages 124-141).

1   Sit in a comfortable position, either cross-legged on the floor or in a chair. Sit up tall with your spine straight, shoulders relaxed and your chest open. Rest your hands on your knees or in your lap with the palms facing up. Relax your face, jaw and stomach. Let your tongue rest on the roof of your mouth, just behind the front teeth. Slightly close your eyes.

2 Breathe slowly, smoothly and deeply in and out through your nose. Breathe deep down into the lowest part of your stomach, all the way down to the perineum. Bring your awareness to the first chakra, located between the tip of the tailbone and the bottom of the pubic bone. Notice any sensations here as you take a few slow, deep breaths in and out.

3 Then inhale and engage your pelvic floor by contracting the muscles between the pubic bone and tailbone and drawing the perineum up towards Muladhara. Keep your focus on feeling the pelvic floor and Muladhara as your breath flows in and your muscles contract. Feel your spine lengthen as your feet and legs push down. If comfortable, hold the breath in for a few seconds. Then release your muscles and exhale the air out through the nose. Repeat for 3-5 minutes, working on increasing the contraction of your pelvic floor if comfortable.

4 Return to a slow deep breath with awareness of Muladhara without engaging the pelvic floor. Feel any sensations here as you take a few slow deep breaths in and out, noticing any changes. Breathe deeply into Muladhara for 3-5 minutes.

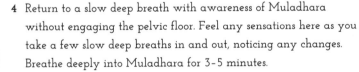

5 To finish, gently let your eyes blink open, inhale with your palms together in front of your heart, exhale and gently bow. Take a moment or two before moving on with the rest of your day.

Outdoors meditation

1 Go outside into your garden or the park, you don't need to be in a beautiful place, all you need is enough space to stand and a little privacy. Take your shoes and socks off and find a spot where you can stand on the grass or bare earth.

2 Stand with your feet shoulder-width apart. When you feel your bare feet connect with the earth, allow each of your vertebrae to stack and rest straight and tall. Close your eyes, consciously soften your shoulders down away from your ears and allow your arms to relax by your sides. With your knees slightly bent, bring your awareness into the soles of your feet.

3 You may become aware of a subtle interplay of energy between the earth and your skin. Notice the weight of your legs and feet pressing down on the ground, and feel that equal and opposite upward force holding you in place. Feel strong and solid. Feel the power in your core; feel the balance at the base of your spine.

4 Breathe in and out, smell the earth and the grass and the fresh air.

5 Gradually allow your awareness to travel up along your body, feeling each body part stacking on top of the part below it, supported by your foundation.

6 When you reach the point where your spinal cord meets the base of your skull, imagine the crown of your head being lifted high into the sky, and rest in this equilibrium for a few minutes. Stand tall. Exist.

7 When you are ready, slowly blink your eyes open, take a moment or two, and get on with your day.

The Second Chakra
SVADHISTHANA

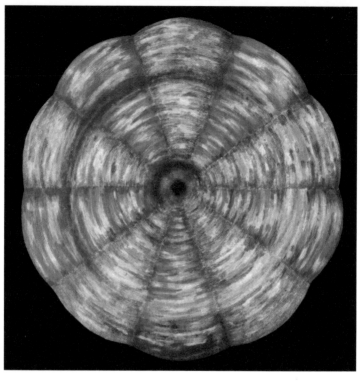

COMMON NAME
The sacral chakra

LOCATION
The sacrum, in the centre of the body below the navel

ELEMENT
Water

COLOUR
Orange

SENSE
Taste

BIJA (SEED) MANTRA
Vam, Om

YANTRA SYMBOL
A six-petalled lotus flower with a circle inside it

ASSOCIATED DEITIES
Indra, Varuna, Vishnu

GEMS AND STONES
Carnelian, fire opal, topaz

The second chakra, Svadhisthana, is located above the pubic bone and below the navel, at the front, and two finger-widths above the coccyx at the back. It sits near the Muladhara chakra, to which it is closely related, both being connected to physical stimuli and interaction. But where memories lie dormant in the first chakra, here in the second they can find expression. While the first chakra is concerned with survival, the second seeks pleasure and enjoyment. If we consider ourselves as vehicles, then the first chakra is the car itself, and the second chakra is the fuel – the passion that fires up the engine so that we can make our dreams come true.

The energy of the sacral chakra allows you to let go ('go with the flow'), to move on, to embrace change and transformation. Translated directly from Sanskrit, Svadhisthana means 'the dwelling place of the self', marking the point when children move on from infancy and begin to develop as individuals. During early teen years, one starts to experience the world through feelings, emotions, pleasure and creativity. For these reasons, the second chakra is often associated with Eric Erikson's second stage of human development.

Your inner child

This chakra governs the flow of creative life-force within us. As humans, it is part of our nature to create. As children in the second stage of development (8 to 14 years), we create in our play, inventing games and characters, colouring, painting, building Lego models, and so on. As we get a little older and become immersed in the education system, we are generally expected to conform, to follow the rules and fit in with others. This can mean that we lose our creative energy. During adulthood, we get used to doing what's right, follow the latest trends, and stick to what is acceptable. This does not encourage creativity. Indeed, blockages of this chakra are common in adults. While you might be happy to undertake a difficult task that you've done before, if asked to draw a picture or cook a meal without a recipe, you might be forced out of your comfort zone. This is because you have stopped being creative, or stopped taking risks creatively because somewhere along the way someone told you couldn't do it. In order to balance your second chakra energy, you need to take risks and not be afraid of failure.

Play is a great way to do this. A child will spend hours building a Lego tower, a sandcastle or a doll's house. That same child will then smash their masterpiece up and start over from scratch as if it was no big deal. Start to play like a child. If your gourmet meal doesn't turn out right, so what? If your potted plant dies in a week, plant another one. And yes, if your work project is a failure, it doesn't mean your career is over. Channel your inner child and, like the child at play, start again. You have an infinite amount of creative energy within you, so use it.

The second chakra is also the well-spring of other aspects of creativity, the raw creativity and passion that artists draw from. But there is creativity in other things too, such as dancing, singing, cooking and gardening. We do each of these things in our own unique way, and they have a beneficial effect on our physical and spiritual selves.

Procreation and the joys of life

Of course, many people express their creativity through procreation and the second chakra's association with the reproductive glands and organs – a woman's womb is situated in the same location – expresses this beautifully on a physical level. Its energy is feminine, passive and lunar. Naturally, the sacral chakra also has a strong connection to sexuality, which is yet another way of letting your life-force flow, experiencing life in a sensual way.

The second chakra is also the centre of pleasure, enjoyment and passion. It allows us to experience life deeply and intensively, as the movement of energy flows through us in the form of sensation, emotion and sensuality. This is one of the strongest forces in us, one that can be difficult to tame. Naturally, it is also considered to be at the root of unconscious desires as an overflow of passion that can transform into an addiction or obsession. Finding the middle-point between a joyful flow of passion and healthy restriction is the balance that a properly working second chakra maintains.

The sacral chakra is associated with the sense of taste, influencing our sensual experience of the world – really tasting it. It expresses our authentic desire to interact with life in a joyful way, to participate in the creative dance of divine energy, to really feel, enjoy and taste being alive.

Balance/imbalance

The second chakra is concerned with our ability to give and receive love. This helps establish a positive identity at the core level of our being, developing a sense of self-worth. It gives us confidence to offer our friendship to others without condition. A person with a balanced second chakra is trustworthy, intuitive and compassionate. They are grounded, open to the world around them, with an emotional stability and a zest for life. In consequence, they are always great company.

As we have seen, the main challenge for the health of your second chakra is social conditioning – we live in a society where, by and large, feelings are not valued, and where passion and emotional reactions are frowned upon. We are taught not to 'lose control' and, over time, can become disconnected from our bodies and our feelings. This chakra is also under threat from cultural attitudes towards sexuality – on the one hand sexuality is magnified and glorified (for example, in advertising) and on the other hand it is repressed and rejected.

Another challenge comes when we lose sight of our inner child, taking on the adult responsibilities of paying the mortgage, bringing up children and looking after ageing parents. During this period of our lives there is little space left for pleasure. We can start losing our sense of play, sensuality and sexuality, and start acting like automatons. As a result, we can suppress our sacral chakra, which becomes underactive. As a consequence we might experience instability, fear of change, sexual dysfunction, depression or addiction.

The yantra and associated deities

The traditional colour associated with the Svadhisthana chakra was vermillion, today it is usually represented as a white lotus with six orange petals. The petals represent six modes of consciousness: *vrittis* (literally 'whirlpools' but here refers to thoughts that swirl through the mind), affection, pitilessness, destructiveness, delusion, disdain and suspicion. Inside the flower there is a circle, representing water, the essence of life.

Symbols in the circle include a silver-coloured crescent moon, which points towards the close relationship between the phases of the moon and the fluctuations of the tides and of human emotions. For some, this symbolism also relates to the feminine menstrual cycle that takes a similar number of days as the phases of the moon to complete, although this is not scientifically correct. However, the connection of the sacral chakra with sexual organs and reproduction is represented by a fish-tailed alligator. This mythical creature is said to represent male sexual power; alligator fat was once used to enhance male virility.

In terms of deities, the second chakra is presided over by Vishnu, the all-pervading life-force in the universe; Varuna, god of the cosmic waters and Indra, god of the heavens, thunder and lightning, storms, rivers and war.

The bija (seed) mantra

The *Upanishads* explain that the five lower chakras are related to the five elements (or *bhutas*) that make up the world: earth (*prithivi*), water (*apas/jala*), fire (*tejas/agni*), air (*vayu*) and ether (*akasha*). Each element has a bija mantra associated with it; when this mantra is sounded it resonates in the chakra and purifies the *nadis* (subtle channels of energy). The *nadis* link the higher spiritual aspects of our being with our mind, emotions and our body. The seed mantra for the Svadhisthana chakra is *vam* (pronounced 'varm', 'vang' or 'fvam'), when spoken it nourishes and purifies bodily fluids and brings alignment with the waters. To create the right noise, start with your upper teeth on your lower lip, and produce a breathy consonant similar to the sound of a car revving, 'fvaarm'. Don't forget that the om chant (see pages 43-44) can be used in healing all the seven main chakras.

Meditations

The following two meditations will start the process of awareness for the second chakra. Should you identify a problem, move on to the yoga *asanas* (see pages 124-141) for help in healing and rebalancing.

1 Sit in a comfortable meditation pose of your choice. Close your eyes. Breathe gently through both nostrils, with your lips sealed. Imagine you are standing by a shallow lake of still water.

2 Imagine that someone drops a large, shiny pebble into the lake. Watch as the ripples grow outwards and disappear.

3 Allow your breath to become progressively shallower, until it is just coming to the end of your nostrils.

4 As your breath becomes calmer, so will your mind. Make sure your breath doesn't make any ripples on the surface of the lake. As the water grows still again, focus all your attention of seeing the pebble on the bed of the lake.

5 If other thoughts start to arise in your mind, do not try to drive them away. The more you try, the more they will return. Become indifferent to these thoughts, focus only on the pebble. The other thoughts will gradually disperse.

6 When the surface of the lake is completely still, you can see to the bottom clearly. When the surface is agitated by ripples or the wind, this is impossible. The same is true of your mind. When it is still, you will experience inner peace.

7 To finish, gently let your eyes blink open, inhale with the palms of your hands over your lower stomach, then exhale gently. Take a moment or two before getting on with the rest of your day.

✳ ✳ ✳

1 Sit or lie in a comfortable position. Ensure that your spine is straight so that energy can flow freely through it.

2 Become aware of your natural breath. How it enters and leaves your body. Where it is in your body. Is it high in your chest? Is it short or long? Don't change it, just observe it.

3 Bring your attention to the location of this chakra, a couple of inches below your belly button.

4 Deepen your breath as you keep your awareness in this area.

5 Visualise a pool of water within your pelvis. A calm and soft body of water. Keep your awareness there as you breathe. Within the body of water is the reflection of a beautiful sunset. The water glows with a beautiful orange hue. Water has the ability to take many forms. From the ocean to the rain, from a flowing river to a deep and still lake. Acknowledge its adaptability. The human body is mostly made from water and is in constant motion (even as you are sitting there in stillness, much is happening on a cellular level) and you are also adaptable.

6 Breathe, be aware of the beauty of the glowing water of the lake. There are no ripples on the water, it is still and the reflection of the sunset is clear. Revel in the scene for a few minutes.

7 To finish, gently let your eyes blink open, inhale with your palms together in front of your lower stomach, then gently exhale.

The Third Chakra
MANIPURA

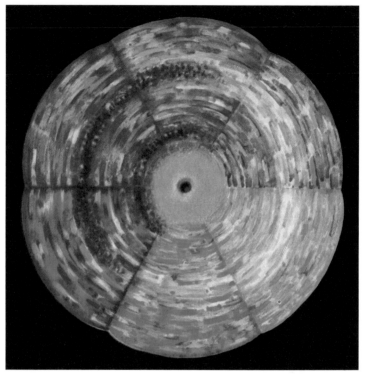

COMMON NAME
The solar plexus chakra

LOCATION
Between the navel
and the bottom of the
sternum

ELEMENT
Fire

COLOUR
Yellow

SENSE
Sight

BIJA (SEED) MANTRA
Ram, Om

YANTRA SYMBOL
A 10-petalled lotus
flower with a
downward pointing
triangle inside it

ASSOCIATED DEITIES
Agni, Vishnu, Lakini

GEMS AND STONES
Topaz, yellow
tourmaline

The third chakra, like the first two, is Earth-based rather than celestial, and deals with what gives us security in our lives. The solar plexus chakra is located above your navel and below your sternum. It functions as the centre of energy associated with ego. It's the source of personal power, self-belief and self-worth. Your solar plexus chakra is activated when you muster the courage to do something that scares you, speak up for yourself or exert your willpower and self-control. You'll notice that in these situations, a balanced third chakra will mean your energy level is high, your posture is tall and commanding, and your voice is firm. However, it's important to note that personal power doesn't mean power over others. It means self-mastery – the ability to master your thoughts and emotions, overcome fear, and take appropriate action in any situation.

The Sanskrit word for the solar plexus is *manipura*, which means 'shining gem' or 'city of jewels'. The chakra contains many of these 'shining gems' in the form of qualities such as clarity, self-confidence, bliss, knowledge, wisdom and the ability to make correct decisions. This chakra is represented as being a vivid golden yellow in colour. Like a ray of sunshine, this chakra lights your path and warms your body with the glow of self-confidence. It is here that we feel our 'gut instinct', the feeling that we get when we are sure of the decision we are about to make. This is also where we feel hollow, some call it 'butterflies', when we are about to do something that makes us nervous, like taking an exam or making a speech.

The explorer

This chakra speaks to your creativity, your personality, your intellect and your ego. According to the ancient traditions, its yellow colour comes from the 'solar' power of the sun and its fire. If it is open and in balance, it will empower you with self-respect and confidence. You will be happy, outgoing, ready to face new challenges with confidence. This is the chakra of the charismatic leader, the explorer. A key element in developing balance for this chakra is understanding yourself.

As you explore the third chakra, you are searching for your personal power, what you want to be in relation to the external world. It is here that you develop the 'self', so that your ego no longer needs the input of others to tell you who you are. For this, you must develop your relationship with yourself. The element of this chakra is fire, and should be used to determine your strength of character. It is personal power and strength of will that you can conquer the inertia that comes from fear and move forward through life. The solar plexus chakra can empower you not to be distracted, to follow your true path.

Criticism and rejection

Self-confidence is a fragile thing and few people can maintain it at all times. Life can sometimes seem full of knocks, put-downs, rejection and disappointments; stress at work or at home can also be debilitating. And it doesn't take much for this chakra to be knocked off balance or even blocked. In fact, criticism and rejection are two of the biggest contributors to a blocked solar plexus chakra. We might start to worry about what others think of us. This can quickly erode self-worth, leading to pessimism and low expectations. A persistent lack of self-confidence can cause people to see themselves as victims, mean that they put up with poor treatment, eroding their resolve to do anything and eventually leading to inertia. Low energy levels, a lack of willpower, and feeling cold emotionally and physically are also indicators of Manipura deficiency.

A closed third chakra can manifest itself as physiological problems too. Due to the location of this chakra in the centre of the body, digestive problems such as indigestion, nausea, ulcers, diabetes, anorexia, coeliac disease and liver disease are associated with a blocked solar plexus chakra.

Getting the balance right

However, balance means that even with self-esteem, calmness and initiative, this chakra also requires respect for others. People with a healthy solar plexus chakra do not boast of their accomplishments – they let their results speak for themselves. They are confident but kind. People who have excessive energy flow to the third chakra are usually overly aggressive. They can be dominating, controlling, manipulative and power-hungry. These people are very competitive. Those with feelings of inadequacy will dramatically overcompensate. This false show of bravado and self-glorification may be seen as confidence or arrogance, but it is false and crumbles easily. This can lead to serious depression and further over-compensatory behaviour. Others are shy and, though they are not prepared to take on a leadership role themselves, are always quick to criticise others. They are also prepared to fail and blame others for their failure.

The key to a healthy solar plexus chakra is finding a balance between being heard without overpowering others with false displays of confidence.

Feel the fear and do it anyway

The fact is that bad things do happen. The important thing is how we deal with them. Do we sink? Do we carry on in an unhealthy relationship? Do we continue to do a job that doesn't use our skills? Does the fear of ageing, balding, obesity or criticism stop us from living our lives? Or do we swim? Do we move forward? Do we find the courage to take risks? Do we 'feel the fear and do it anyway'? A healthy, balanced third chakra will show us the way forward.

As we have discussed, a lack of self-confidence (perhaps consistent in certain areas of your life or following a traumatic incident or even simply after suffering one of life's regular knock-backs) is a common issue that most of us face regularly. Inertia might be a short-term issue for you. Why not try one or more of the following things to get yourself going? Start slowly and build up:

* Do exercises designed to strengthen your core: crunches, sit-ups, the mountain climber, the plank and leg raises

* Dance

* Practice yoga

* Eat yellow foods such as bananas, corn, grains (see page 144)

* Drink herbal teas

* Wear yellow and introduce yellow accents into your home environment

* Encourage yourself to step out of your comfort zone by changing your daily routine

* Seek out new experiences and unexplored wisdom to expand your repertoire of knowledge and skills

Take chances, take yourself out of your comfort zone. Your natural confidence will begin to re-emerge. It might be a little scary at first, but it focuses us to be in the moment and stop overthinking. Let your actions speak for themselves, and find the courage to act by focusing on your strengths and taking small proactive steps.

The yantra and associated deities

The use of yantras as an aid to meditation is widespread. They are said to be symbolic representations of divine or cosmic forces, a window into the Absolute. When the mind is concentrated on a single, simple object, it helps clear mental chatter, allowing it to remain empty and silent and to permit contemplation of higher thoughts. The ten shining yellow lotus petals of this yantra correspond to the *vrittis* (whirlpools of thought) of jealousy, spiritual ignorance, thirst, treachery, fear, shame, disgust, foolishness, delusion and sadness, and the ten *pranas*, the vital forces that control and nourish all functions of the human body. They also refer to our ability to manipulate our surroundings, often via the ten fingers on our hands. Inside the circle of petals is a fiery-red downward-pointing triangle, which indicates the spreading of energy, growth and development. Inside the triangle is the symbol of the seed mantra. It also has three T-shaped projections (called *svastikas*) indicating movement. Below the triangle is a ram, a powerful and energetic animal representing the strength and power of who we are in the world. The deities associated with this chakra are Agni, the god of fire; Vishnu, symbolic of human consciousness, and his partner Lakini, who is able to dispel fear and grant boons.

The bija (seed) mantra

A mantra works in a similar way to a tuning fork. As the tuning fork rings out a note it vibrates and, as we use our vocal cords to make certain sounds, so they too vibrate. These vibrations channel cosmic energy through our bodies, which generate healing powers. The aim of these seed mantras is to help us get onto the frequency that relates to each particular chakra. The seed mantra for the third chakra is *ram*, pronounced 'rang'. The 'r' is produced with the tip of the tongue curling up to the roof of your mouth. When you get the sound right you will feel the mantra resonating from the navel. The sound is said to assist longevity. If you find the mantras useful for you, don't forget that the om chant (Pages 43-44) is an effective healing method for all seven of the main chakras so try using both during your meditation sessions.

Meditations

1 Choose a quiet place, in the garden or the park. Stand tall, ideally in the sun, and close your eyes.

2 With your arms by your sides, take a few moments to turn your attention inward. When your breathing is steady and unhurried, notice the ground beneath your feet and the space above your head.

3 Breathing in, slowly draw your arms up to the sky; visualise a bright yellow flame igniting in the core of your abdomen. As you exhale, lower your arms in one fluid motion.

4 Continue this flow, feeling the chakra colour grow bigger and more vibrant with every inhale. As you connect with the Earth beneath you and the astral world above you, feel the perfect equilibrium in which you exist.

5 When the shining yellow light has engulfed your entire body, keep your arms overhead and breathe, embracing a strong sense of your personal power and dosing yourself generously with healthy self-esteem.

6 When you are ready, slowly blink your eyes open. Give yourself a moment and then get on with the rest of your day.

✹ ✹ ✹

1 Light a candle or a tealight or two if you are indoors and especially if it is dark.

2 Sit down in a comfortable position for meditation.

3 Cup your left hand and make a fist with your right hand, extending your right thumb up. Place your right fist in your left palm, and draw your hands in front of your solar plexus (just below the sternum and above the navel). Close your eyes. Connect to the rise and fall of your breath.

4 Imagine that your right thumb is a flame, flickering at the centre of your being. With each inhale that you take, watch the yellow flame grow a little bit brighter. Imagine a warmth spreading from this area of your body and filling you from the inside out.

5 Now, imagine that you have gathered a little stack of sticks. On each stick, write a word or phrase representing something in your life that is no longer serving you, something that you are in the process of letting go, or need to be. Remember that some things must be let go of hundreds of times before we are free from them. Forgive yourself this process, because letting go is one of the hardest things to do.

6 Now, place each stick into your flame. Watch it catch fire. And burn. And as each stick is completely burned, imagine that a gust of wind travels into your hands and carries the ash away from you, far, far away.

7 Ask yourself: Do I have the energy to do the things I want to do? Do I have the confidence to do the things I want to do? What gets in the way? Often, our energy is drained in one area of our life, and we are left lifeless for the mountain of wonderful, enriching experiences that could be.
Breathe.

8 Connect to the rise and fall of your breath. When you are ready, blink your eyes open, take a moment before going back to your day.

The Fourth Chakra
ANAHATA

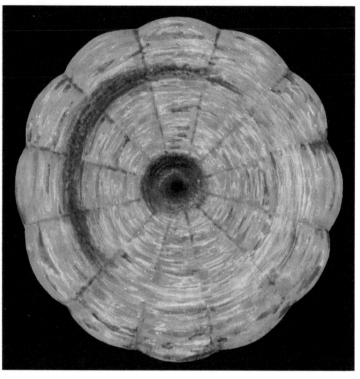

COMMON NAME
The heart chakra

LOCATION
The cardiac plexus,
including the heart,
lungs and thymus gland

ELEMENT
Air

COLOUR
Green

SENSE
Touch

BIJA (SEED) MANTRA
Lam, Om

YANTRA SYMBOL
A circle of 12 lotus
petals, inside which is a
six-pointed star

ASSOCIATED DEITIES
Rudra, Vayu, Kakini

GEMS AND STONES
Emerald, jade, peridot,
rose quartz

The heart sits at the centre of our bodies, it pumps out our life blood, it beats out the rhythm of our lives. It is also the seat of love, the greatest power we have on the Earth. It is through love that we really live, it is through love that we build relationships that make us whole. Without the heart, there is no health, no healing. Without the heart and its love, life is meaningless and we wither and die. Everything begins and ends with love. Love is free, abundant and limitless. Anahata, the central chakra, unifies the physical chakras below and those of the spirit above. As a consequence, it is the most important chakra of all.

The heart chakra is the wheel of energy located at the level of the sternum, or breastbone. It encompasses the heart, lungs, sternum, clavicle, shoulder blades, breast tissue, thymus gland and rib cage. The arms and hands are also extensions of this chakra. The heart is made of a unique type of muscle tissue called cardiac muscle. This allows the heart to beat without getting tired. Cardiac muscle has a higher percentage of mitochondria – the power sources of the cells – than skeletal muscle and so it does not fatigue.

But this tireless service cannot happen unless the heart itself is nourished first. When the oxygen-rich blood leaves the heart it travels through the aorta and out into the body. The first branch off of the aorta is back to the muscles of the heart itself. The first thing the heart does is nourish itself. It serves the entire body every day, for our whole life, but it will always take care of its own needs first.

Love and judgement

When we think of love, it is easy to be trite: perhaps we think about innocent babies, or puppies or kittens. Perhaps we think of twee images of kids with big eyes or stock phrases like 'love means never having to say you're sorry'. We might also think of steamy sex that we've already had or are looking forward to. But these concepts are not really sustainable over time. Babies and puppies grow, statistically the 'in love' feeling of a romantic relationship lasts about two years and is part of your primeval need to make sure the human race continues.

The heart has more spiritual concerns. Just as it nourishes itself first, so it allows us to love ourselves first, then to love others, to let others love us, and to give and receive love from all of humanity.
What the heart really wants is unconditional love and that is a challenge; the challenge to sustain this feeling through the grind of daily life after those initial two years, to love those we judge and to love ourselves. It is only when you have love and compassion for yourself, that you can truly love others in a healthy, happy and healing way.

The heart's message is that you can't really help others unless you help yourself. If we judge and condemn our frailties and our faults, as we do those of others, we will find it hard to love. If a mother dedicates herself wholly to her child and takes no rest or nourishment for herself, then both she and the child will suffer. If a doctor spends too much time with patients and not enough on rest, then mistakes might result. A balanced heart chakra must begin with self-care.

Compassion and forgiveness

As we journey through the vicissitudes of our emotional lives, we should seek balance. When the heart chakra is balanced it allows us to experience feelings of compassion, selflessness and healing. The world revolves around ourselves and our feelings. Compassion helps us realise that we are not the only ones suffering, it reminds us that we are all in the same boat. This unifies us, connecting us with the whole of humanity. If the heart is too weak, we lack trust and disconnect from others. If it is too open then we can easily be overwhelmed by sympathy for others. Over-attachment can make us desperate for connections, a need for detachment might make us push people away rather than risk being vulnerable. The solution is to recognise our own human-ness, accept our faults and failings as well as those of others, to trust that the need for love and compassion will be met.

In terms of romantic love and friendship, it is impossible to avoid situations where someone might hurt you. When you get hurt, you have several choices. You can live in the place of grievances, unable to forgive. You can hold on to the bad feelings, develop anger, bitterness and resentment. As well as depression, physical afflictions caused by the blockage in the fourth chakra can include cardiac disease, arrhythmia, pneumonia, asthma, allergies and lung conditions. Or you can look that pain in the face, feel it and then let it go. Your mind and your ego might tell you otherwise, but it really is as simple as that.

The Sanskrit name for the heart chakra, Anahata, means 'unhurt', 'unstruck' or 'unbeaten'. Symbolically, this means that beneath the hurts and grievances of past experiences lies a pure and spiritual place where no hurt exists.

The yantra and associated deities

The anahata yantra features a lotus flower with 12 lustrous green petals, which match the divine qualities of the heart. In the centre are two overlapping, intersecting triangles, making a shape known as a *shatkona* and resembling the Star of David. The six points of the star are said to represent the other six chakras. The triangle facing upwards symbolises Shiva, the male principle, matter rising to meet spirit. The other triangle, facing downward, symbolises Shakti, the female principle, as spirit descends to inhabit the body. A balance is attained when these two forces are joined in harmony; this is the source of all creation. Inside the central part of the shatkona is the symbol for the seed mantra *yam*, and a golden triangle indicating the divine light that can be revealed when the chakra is fully opened. Inside that, a crescent moon lights the path to enlightenment and shows the psychic blocks that must be dissolved to achieve it. The chakra's associated animal is the black antelope or gazelle, symbolising the lightness, speed and freedom of the fourth chakra's element, air. The goddess presiding over this chakra is Kakini, who synchronises the beat of our hearts with the beat of the cosmos. The presiding deity is Rudra, the manifestation of Shiva, while seed mantra yam (see below) is believed to be the sound form of Vayu, lord of the wind.

The bija (seed) mantra

The name mantra is taken from the Sanskrit words *man*, meaning 'to think' and *tra*, meaning 'liberate'. The use of mantras for help in meditation was adopted by Hatha yoga practitioners for use in keeping focus during their sessions. They are of particular help in keeping your mind focused on your breath. Chanting a mantra during practice can help to reduce your *chitta vritti*, or mind chatter. The seed mantra for the heart chakra is *yam* (pronounced 'yarm' or 'yang'). Anahata is the centre of the seven main chakras, where the physical body and the spiritual body meet. Therefore it affects both physical and spiritual well-being. The mantra gives control over the breath and is said to promote love, compassion and forgiveness. Always remember that you can prolong your mantra session by chanting om, the most sacred syllable symbol and mantra of Brahman, the Almighty God in Hinduism, creator of all existence.

Meditations

1   Sit in a comfortable position, either cross-legged on the floor or in a chair. Sit up tall with your spine straight, your shoulders relaxed and your chest open. Hold your palms together and lightly press the knuckles of the thumbs into the sternum at the level of your heart (you should feel a little notch where the knuckles magically fit). Breathe slowly, smoothly and deeply into your stomach and chest. Lightly close your eyes.

2   Let go of any thoughts or distractions and let your mind focus on feeling the breath moving in and out of your body. Once your mind feels quiet and still, bring your focus to the light pressure of the thumbs pressing against your chest and feel the beating of your heart. Keep this focus for a few minutes.

3   Then, gently release your hands and rub the palms together, making them warm and energised. Place your right palm in the centre of your chest and your left hand on top of your right. Close your eyes and feel the centre of your chest warm and radiant, full of energy. See this energy as an emerald green light, radiating out from the centre of your heart into the rest of your body. Feel this energy flowing out into your arms and hands, and flowing back

into the heart. Stay with this visualisation for a few minutes.

4 When you feel completely soaked with heart chakra energy, gently release your palms and turn them outwards with the elbows bent, the shoulders relaxed and the chest open. Feel or visualize the green light love energy flowing out of your palms and into the world. You can direct it towards specific loved ones in your life or to all sentient beings.

5 To end your meditation, inhale as you push your arms up towards the sky, connecting with the heavens, then exhale and lower the palms lightly to the floor, connecting with the earth. Take a moment or two before moving on with the rest of your day.

1 Sit down in a comfortable position. Soften and then close your eyes and allow your mind to relax. Sit tall with your spine and neck long and your shoulders relaxed. Begin to focus on your breath. As you inhale and exhale, focus on different parts of your body and release any tension you feel there.

2 Let go of your thoughts for a moment, feel yourself deeply relaxed. Then focus your attention on your heart. Think of it as a space and feel the breath enter and leave that space. Feel your heart safe, secure and relaxed.

3 Your heart is a point of awareness, the point where feelings enter. Feel whatever is in there, it might be peace, it might be light, you might feel stress, disappointment or longing. Don't strain to find anything, just feel whatever is in there, allow it to just be.

4 Keeping your attention there, breathe gently, sense the breath flowing through your heart. Visualise a soft, pastel light or coolness pervading the chest. Now imagine that with each nurturing and nourishing breath, you're wiping away any dirt or dust that's covering your heart. Imagine that your breath is actually inhaling into the heart and exhaling out of the heart. Be here, with this breath for several moments.

5 As you breathe, ask your heart if it wants to say something. For the next few minutes, sit and listen for an answer. It may stay silent and at peace, but it may release emotions, memories, fears and dreams long stored inside. This may release strong emotions, a quickness of breath, even tears. Whatever happens, let the experience be what it is. If you drift off to sleep or daydream, don't worry. Just bring back your attention to your heart.

6 When you're ready, open your eyes and bring your hands and palms together at your heart centre. Bow to your heart and tell it you'll be with it again soon. Thank it for its loving wisdom and daily guidance.

The Fifth Chakra
VISHUDDHA

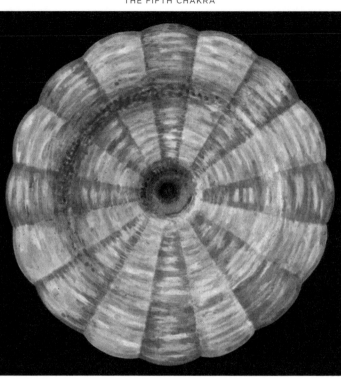

COMMON NAME
The throat chakra

LOCATION
The throat, thyroid, parathyroid, jaw, neck, mouth, tongue and larynx

ELEMENTS
Sound/space/ether

COLOUR
Bright blue

SENSE
Hearing

BIJA (SEED) MANTRA
Ham, Om

YANTRA SYMBOL
A circle of 16 lotus petals, inside which is a downward pointing triangle

ASSOCIATED DEITIES
Ganga, Sarasvati

GEMS AND STONES
Sapphire, blue topaz, aquamarine, lapis lazuli

The fifth chakra, Vishuddha, is the chakra of communication. Human communication in terms of languages, words and sentences is something that distinguishes us from other species. This use of language is a gift, but one that can be used to heal and harm. Having a voice allows us to express ourselves, to our family, to our friends, to everyone. It gives us self-expression, the right to speak and be heard, a voice in the world. It allows to say what is in our heart and soul. It makes us who we are. With communication comes sound, the primary element of this chakra.

The word vishuddha is Sanskrit for 'purification' or 'pure wisdom', and a major challenge of this energy centre is in finding the wisdom to determine how to communicate in ways that do justice to you, to others and to any higher consciousness or higher being. In consequence, this is the first of the three spiritual chakras. It sits at the centre of the neck, and forms the passage between the body and the head. It is said to be the bridge between our hearts and our minds, our bodies and our spirits.

When blocked, this chakra can make you tongue-tied and unable to express your feelings. You may find that your ability to attract what you want is hampered by an inability to use the right words at the right time. When functioning well, you are able to maintain a strong, balanced relationship with those around you and with the higher realms. Mantras are often used in order to ensure that this chakra is operating to the best of its ability.

Speaking and listening

Communication involves both speaking and listening. The major life forces of this chakra are sound, vibration and resonance. In order to verbalise our ideas, we must pay attention to how we say the words. Your voice is not merely words, but how you say them. Babies and dogs don't understand the words you say, but through the rhythm and resonance of the sound, they will understand the message. Our voices resonate with the sound of the language we use, so if we speak in a clear and inviting way, others will pick up the rhythm, hearing that and hearing what we actually say.

Of course, it's not always that easy. Authentic expression is not something that comes easily. There's a delicate dance between saying what you mean and being tactful. It's often easier to say what you think the other person may want to hear instead of speaking the truth. Fear of not being accepted, or judgment from the other may hinder your truthful verbal expression.

Listening is another aspect of the fifth chakra. The highest form of listening does not mean shutting up and thinking about the next point you are going to make, while pretending to listen when the other person is talking. It means giving the other person your full attention and really hearing what they say. This might even mean putting away your mobile or turning your computer off and waiting to hear the other person completely before responding.

Telling the truth

Work on the lower chakras will help prepare you for this. When you align the first and second chakras, it helps with overcoming fear. Opening the third chakra helps you to feel your personal power and have the confidence to express yourself. Knowing what's in your heart comes when you align the fourth chakra. Then, when it comes to verbalising your needs, desires and opinions, you're better able to determine how to be truthful to yourself and others. It is to this process that the word *vishuddha*, 'purifier', refers.

Dr David Simon, a world-renowned authority in the field of mind-body medicine, often quoted the following ancient wisdom. He said that there are three gateways you should cross before speaking:

* First, ask yourself, 'Is what I am about to say true?'

* If so, proceed to the second gateway and ask, 'Is what I am about to say necessary?'

* If the answer is yes, go to the third gateway and ask yourself, 'Is what I am about to say kind?'

Speaking your highest truth doesn't mean you're allowed to be hurtful or critical. The truth from your spiritual essence will come across as kind and compassionate.

Between the heart and the head

In the *Descent of Man* (1871), Charles Darwin had a theory that human voices developed when chest and throat muscles contracted in excitement or fear, suggesting that voice and emotion come from the same impulse. Might this be why a lump in the throat is often the first sign of emotional distress? When someone feels anxiety or tension, their speaking voice is affected. Of course, the opposite is true. Your mood can be lifted by chanting and through yoga poses, for example, and many people swear by the restorative effects of singing, particularly singing in a choir. Biologists tell us that this is because of breathing, the release of endorphins, and because singing gets more oxygen to the blood.

But there is more to it than that, singing touches something deep inside us. Why is it that all spiritual practices sing hymns or mantras? They are used to clear the mind and help us to unite with a divine entity. Ann Dyer, a yoga instructor and singer, explains: 'The voice lies between the heart and the head. So, on a very basic level, the act of chanting brings together your intellectual awareness with your heart awareness.' This idea is backed up by another singing yogi, Suzanne Sterling, who explains that, 'At the molecular level, we are vibrating entities,' and because the voice is a vibration it communicates directly with our core. When we allow certain tones to run through our bodies, it can bring us back to harmony.

Western medicine is catching on to this idea too and listening to music is recognised as a part of therapy and pain and stress management. Studies carried out during the last thirty years have proved that singing can have both physical and psychological benefits. Ann Dyer recommends yoga and daily chanting. 'The more familiar your voice becomes to you,' she says, 'the more it will begin to reveal your truest self.' Your state of being is reflected in your voice, or as she calls it, 'the barometer of your being'.

A healthy and well-balanced fifth chakra will enable you to express yourself, though your voice, in a manner that is nurturing both for yourself and for others. Those who speak too softly may be unable to speak their truth or may be oppressed in some way. Those who shout are clearly not listening to others, and their conversations are most likely to be rather short. They would do well to take notice of the saying that 'in order to be a great conversationalist, try listening'. There are many symptoms of an unbalanced Vishuddha chakra, including a stiff neck, sore throat, blocked ears, swollen glands and laryngitis.

Yantra and associated deities

The yantra symbol for Vishuddha is a sixteen-petal lotus around a white circle, thought to represent the full moon or the element ether. On each petal is a letter from the Sanskrit alphabet through which communication is possible. Within this circle is a silver crescent, the symbol of the cosmic sound *nadam* (the 'inner music' that we hear when we stop

chanting), indicating purity in the sound of silence. There is also a downward pointing triangle, *akasa mandala*, which represents Shakti, the female power of creation. Inside the triangle is the symbol for the seed mantra *ham*. Below them is the elephant with the seven trunks, Alravata, also present in the Muladhara yantra, who serves all the major chakras with his strength and power. The deity that governs the fifth chakra is Sarasvati, the goddess of flow, speech, knowledge and the arts, while Ganga (named after the river Ganges), symbolises the purification of sins granted to those who bathe in its waters every day.

The bija (seed) mantra

Mantras, particularly single syllable bija mantras, are usually chanted for their healing sound vibrations, rather than any specific meaning. They are thought to clear the subtle energy pathways in the body in order to create positive change. Chant the bija mantras, either one at a time or in sequence. Used in sequence with the chakras, they will resonate up and down the spine. The first sound (consonant) should be shorter than the second, and the final sound, usually 'm' or 'n' should be held for longer. Repetition can help you access a meditative state. The bija mantra for the vishuddha chakra is *ham* (pronounced 'hum' or 'hang'). The 'h' sound is produced at the back of the throat. This chant is said to energise the throat and the brain, bringing sweetness and harmony to your voice. If chanting is helpful for you, you can extend the session by using the om chant (see pages 43-44), which is helpful in opening all of your chakras. The two chants can even be sung together, as in 'aumhum'.

Meditation

1 Sit down in a comfortable position. Shut your eyes and take a long,
   deep breath. As you exhale, move your attention to your throat
   and imagine a sapphire-blue chakra. The blue glow of the chakra
   spreads like a vibration or a pulse from your throat to fill your
   neck and head first and then the rest of your body.

2 Imagine walking through a forest on a narrow path that is lined
   on both sides by huge shade-giving trees. You hear the sounds of
   insects, of small animals scurrying around and of chirping birds. In
   the distance, a stream flowing over its rocky bed makes a pleasant
   gurgling sound.

3 You find a small clearing in which a giant log has fallen on
   the forest floor. You walk up to it and sit with your back resting
   against the log.

4 The sounds of the forest become even more evident to you. There
   is a magical quality to them and you can now hear the faintest of
   sounds. The whole forest is playing a symphony, especially for you.

5 Now see your fifth chakra spinning and gaining strength. As it
   spins faster, a blue light washes over you and pervades every cell,
   every pore in your body.

6 Breathe deeply and feel the energy funnelling into your throat, which is bursting with dazzling blue light. Rest in this awareness.

7 Gently stand up and start walking back from the clearing to the edge of the forest, where you first started. Look back at the singing forest and feel at one with it.

8 When you are ready, open your eyes, stand up and get on with the rest of your day.

Second throat meditation

1 Sit in a chair with your feet flat on the floor, or on a cushion, wherever you feel comfortable. Slowly blink your eyes closed. Bring your awareness to your breath. Notice the rise and fall of your chest, the natural rhythm of your breathing. Sit and breathe for a few moments.

2 If you find your thoughts wandering, let them. Welcome the thoughts, then gently let them go by coming back to this meditation. Now, make two or three deep yawns. You can 'fake yawn' until a real one comes along. Then bring your attention back to the breath. Notice the natural rhythm of your breathing.

3   At the base of the throat is your throat chakra. Imagine that it is a tiny sky-blue light, spinning. With each breath, grow this blue light. Expand it first to your neck. Then expand again to the mouth, then the ears, then your entire head.

4   Take another breath and continue to expand this light. Expand until it is all around you and you are in a bubble of blue light. Hold that light all around you for three breaths. Focus this beautiful blue light back on the throat. Coat the throat with the light, both inside and out. Illuminate the voice box, the thyroid and all around the neck. Send this light to your mouth to coat your teeth, tongue, and lips. This light expands to your ears, awakening your ability to listen. This light heals all these areas as it moves over them. Breathe in the light.

5   Keep your eyes closed or hooded as you near the end of this meditation. It's important to come out of meditation slowly. Bring your awareness back to the breath. Allow yourself to feel the in and out rhythm of the rise and fall of the breath.

6   On your next inhale, wiggle your fingers and toes. Gently shift your arms or legs as needed.

7   When you're ready, open your eyes with a soft downward gaze. Keep your focus inward. Open your eyes fully when you're ready.

The Sixth Chakra
AJNA

COMMON NAME
The brow or third-eye chakra

LOCATION
The centre of the head, between and slightly above the level of the eyebrows

ELEMENT
Light

COLOUR
Deep blue/indigo

SENSE
Sight

BIJA (SEED) MANTRA
Om

YANTRA SYMBOL
Two white lotus petals around a circle, inside which is a downward-pointing triangle

ASSOCIATED DEITIES
Shiva, Hakini Shakti

GEMS AND STONES
Diamonds, emeralds, sapphire

The sixth chakra is located in the area of the third eye, which is found in the space between and slightly above the eyebrows. It encompasses the pituitary gland, the eyes, head and the lower part of the brain. An invisible yet powerful third eye, this is your centre of intuition, often known as the 'seat of the soul'. It is a metaphorical eye, often marked on a Hindu's forehead with a red dot. Ajna, which in Sanskrit means 'beyond wisdom', is a spiritual chakra and, if you let it, it will lead you to an inner knowledge.

A current theme in spiritual teaching is that the world is an illusion, and that you must search through the dogma – from our culture, politics and social structures – to arrive at your own personal truth. But this is easier said than done. After all, we can all see solutions to others' problems more easily than we can see our own. Our left brain also does a great job of hiding inner truth from our consciousness. How often do you find yourself thinking, 'Oh, that can't possibly happen', moments before it does? We have an innate ability to rationalise everything so that we can stay in our comfort zones and continue to believe in our illusions, even though they are often based on fear. Deep inside us all, we hope that there is a better and higher way of being. One without fear of making mistakes or doing wrong and instead filled with joy and happiness. What we must do to find this is take notice of the truths we see through our third eye, the chakra of wisdom and intuition.

Your 'sixth sense'

Even before birth, a baby starts to experience the world through its physical senses: hearing its mother's heartbeat, listening to muffled sounds, tasting, touching, and even seeing degrees of light. By the time you are born, you have already learned to trust these senses. While they are essential tools for life in the physical world, they are of little use in a person's spiritual life.

While your physical eyes see things through the reflection of light (without light, the physical eye does not see at all), your third eye 'sees' beyond the physical, going into the world of imagination, visualisation and clairvoyance. The third eye sees using a different kind of light, the shining light of spiritual insight.

Before the advent of modern technology, intuition was an essential tool. Humans had more reason to rely on their primal instincts and signals from the environment to guide them. Just like birds are said to know when an earthquake is about to occur and cats know when it's time for dinner even though they can't read a clock, so humans have an intuitive 'sixth' sense. We've all heard stories of people having hunches that turn out to be correct, or saying 'I felt that someone was following me', or 'Something about it didn't feel quite right'. More often than not though, we ignore the feeling. This is because we have lost touch with intuition and our ability to trust it.

Decisions, decisions

Trusting in your inner sense is a huge help in making decisions. This is not a fail-safe method but it means continuing to use your mind, your intellect and your ego, as usual, but adding your soul to the decision-making process. The best help will come from a healthy Ajna chakra. Like all the spiritual chakras, it is best balanced through meditation. Someone with an open and balanced third eye chakra is better able to separate truth from illusion, thereby developing trust in their inner wisdom. Using the mindful skills developed in this emotional centre, allows the person to receive guidance and inspiration from their creativity and intuition. This is emotional intelligence and allows the individual to evaluate both their conscious and unconscious insights to reach the best decision.

Excessive energy in this chakra can cause difficulties with concentration, headaches, nightmares and even hallucinations. An overactive third eye chakra can also, in some cases, lead to severe emotional disturbances, such as schizophrenia. Deficiencies show themselves as poor memory, eye problems, difficulty recognising problems, and not being able to visualise well. In the modern world we often suffer from these problems due to the busy lives we lead. Too much time looking at computer screens, social media and rushing from here to there can affect our ability to focus or switch off. Having time away from these all-encompassing technologies and just sitting with yourself can recharge your third eye chakra and, in turn, help you when you need to concentrate, relax or sleep.

The yantra and associated deities

The lotus flower of the Ajna yantra has only two white petals, which sit on each side of a white circle. These are variously represented as wings, our physical eyes and the topmost point where the Ida and Pingala *nadis* (channels) that carry our *prana* (life force) meet. This reminds us of the duality in all things – the highest point at which our rising vitality and our descending energy meet. The white circle represents the void, which exists beyond the five senses. Inside the circle, a crescent moon represents the Ajna vortex and a red dot shows how the body is able to rise above the sexual energy of the body symbolised by the upside down triangle below. The triangle also symbolises wisdom, the yoni (female sexual organ) and the trinity of the godhead. Inside it is the symbol of the mantra, om, and a lingam (male sexual organ). Deities associated with this yantra are Shiva and Hakini Shakti, the aspect of the feminine divine linked to this chakra.

The bija (seed) mantra

Om (pronounced 'aum', see page 43-44) is the most renowned and expansive of the bija mantras. It is the mantra of assent and the form of creation, causing energy to surge upward and outward. It is used with the sixth chakra because chanting it is said to be able to open the third eye by physically merging the left and right hemispheres of the brain. According to Paramahansa Yogananda (author of *Autobiography of a Yogi*). 'Om or Aum of the *Vedas* became the sacred word *Hum* of the Tibetans, *Amin* of the Muslims and *Amen* of the Egyptians, Greeks, Romans, Jews and Christians.' The word has been translated into many different languages, cultures and religious traditions, but the creative and transformative power of the sound remains the same.

Meditations

Meditation is the most effective way of opening the third eye chakra. But people have different reactions to the process. Some experience flashing images of things they are familiar with: nature, waterfalls, people and trains, for example. Others describe it as being able to see your thoughts, almost as if they are scrolling by on a blackboard.

It is common to have a headache during your first attempts to activate the third eye. Don't worry – as you continue to practice the headaches will go away. To train yourself to more fully appreciate the third eye, try focusing on one particular image. It could be a number, it could be an object – just try to keep your mind centred on whatever image you have chosen.

If you aren't able to get in touch with the third eye immediately, don't worry. Meditation can take a while to get used to, and activating the third eye even longer.

1   Sit down in comfortable manner for meditation. Slowly blink your eyes closed. Take a few long and deep breaths. As you exhale, bring your attention to the centre of your forehead, in between the brows and just above the brow line, and imagine an indigo-blue chakra. Watch as the dark indigo glow of the chakra illuminates your mind and then spreads to the rest of your body.

2   Imagine an entrance to your mind through the third eye. Open the door and walk into an empty room. Imagine the room any way you like - choose the colour, decor, look and feel. Make it suit your tastes perfectly, so that it becomes your personal sanctuary.

3 Find the most comfortable spot in the room and sit down. Look out onto the world from there. Bring into focus the same thoughts, issues, situations and ideas that occupy your day-to-day life. Silently contemplate them.

4 Now imagine your sixth chakra spinning and gaining strength. As it spins faster, its indigo light washes over you and pervades every cell, every pore in your body.

5 Breathe deeply and feel the energy bursting from your third eye as rays of dazzling deep blue light.

6 Rest in this awareness for a few moments, gazing at the world in this new, clean light.

7 When you are finished, gently stand up and walk to the door through which you entered the room. Walk out and look back at your inner sanctuary and feel one with it before closing the door. Then imagine returning to your body. Breathe.

8 When you are ready, blink your eyes open, stand up and get on with your day.

✻ ✻ ✻

1 Sit down in a comfortable position for meditation. Slowly blink your eyes closed. Keep your head up, your chest open and your back straight. Place your hands in your lap or your knees.

2 Breathe in and out. Be mindful of your body and how it feels in the moment. If there are aches in your body, work on relaxing those before you begin. Focus on each part of your body in turn as you sit and relax.

3 When you are ready, focus on the present moment. Feel your body expand and contract with each breath. Be aware of how your breath goes in and out. Try to focus entirely on your breathing. Take a deep breath (inhale for a count of three, then exhale for a count of three), repeat with two more deep breaths.

4 When you are ready, start focusing on your third eye at the centre of your forehead. Under your eyelids, move your eyes up toward the third eye. Keep them focused there throughout the meditation. Begin counting backwards from one hundred.

5 By the time you have reached zero, you should be ready to access the third eye. If you are properly focused, everything will be dark except the third eye. Your brain will be relaxed but functioning at a new level. Both sides of the brain will be working together and you will be aware of the energy around you.

6   You can also tell if your third eye has been activated when you are able to focus strongly on just one object and your mind is completely consumed by holding that image. Stay in that moment for a while.

7   When you are ready, bring yourself slowly out of the meditation. Move your eyes away from the third eye. Stay relaxed, but become more aware of your breath. Be mindful of the way that your breath goes in and out. Sometimes counting helps to put more focus on your breath as you are coming out of your meditation. Blink your eyes open and return to your day.

The Seventh Chakra
SAHASRARA

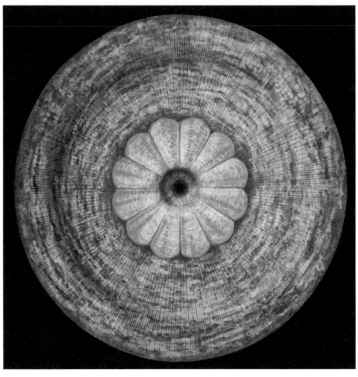

COMMON NAME
The crown chakra

LOCATION
The top of the head

ELEMENT
Thought

COLOUR
Violet

SENSE
None

BIJA (SEED) MANTRA
Silence/Om

YANTRA SYMBOL
1,000-petalled lotus
flower, the petals, of
different colours, are
arranged in 20 layers

with 50 petals in
each layer. Inside is
an upward-pointing
triangle

ASSOCIATED DEITIES
Shiva, Shakti

GEMS AND STONES
Sapphire, amethyst,
celestite

The seventh and last chakra, Sahasrara, is unlike the others in several ways. Most importantly, it sits outside the body and is therefore not directly associated with the physical. Some say it sits on top of the head, others that it is slightly above, both descriptions explain its common name of the crown chakra. Unlike the other chakras, Sahasrara does not affect specific aspects of our lives. If your seventh chakra is unbalanced you are unlikely to notice any physical symptoms. Unlike the others, healing this chakra does not require a difficult yoga *asana*, or the chanting of a specific mantra (although some associate om with Sahasrara). Instead it requires nothing but silence, meditation and patient waiting…

This is also the hardest chakra to introduce to the beginner. For many, in this task-focused modern digital age, talk of spiritual development, enlightenment and living in a state of pure awareness can be hard to take seriously. It can be difficult to reconcile the pursuit of awareness of a higher consciousness with the demands of our daily lives. Cynicism is the most likely response. But you can think about it in another way. In our own ways, we have all had moments of joy, of extreme happiness, of clarity, of contentment. Can these not be described as 'moments of pure awareness'? Practicing meditation, prayer if you want to do it, and daily silence are disciplines that lead to increased moments of spiritual connection and longer moments of pure awareness. The more you practice these, the better you will get.

The brain, the mind and the universe

Because of its location on top of the head, the crown chakra is closely associated with the brain and the endocrine system, notably the pineal and pituitary glands. The endocrine system is the collection of glands that produce hormones regulating growth and development, tissue function, metabolism, sexual function, reproduction, sleep and mood among other things. The brain is the centre of the nervous system. Physiologically, it works like a big computer, processing information that it receives from the senses and the body, and sending messages back to the body. It is the most complex organ in the human body and exerts centralised control over all the other organs.

The brain's statistics are astonishing: it contains approximately 86 billion nerve cells (neurons), each one capable of transmitting 1,000 impulses per second, which travel at the same speed as Formula One cars. A piece of brain tissue the size of a grain of sand contains 100,000 neurons and a billion synapses, all communicating with each other. There are 100,000 miles of blood vessels in the brain – the distance around the world at the equator is 24,900 miles! The brain plays a key role in how we are able to pay attention, our perception, awareness, thought, memory and language. But even these facts pale into insignificance when you think that the brain contains your consciousness. Your consciousness is made up of everything you have experienced in your life: your memories, your loves, your likes and dislikes, and the knowledge that one day it will end. It is astonishing to think that, at every moment, you carry everything with you inside your head. Your mind has no limits, no time constraints, no connection to the material world and no locality. Sahasrara represents that freedom – no wonder we should look after it.

Internal quiet

Experiencing Sahasrara is a rare thing. But looking for, and finding, quiet moments of liberation, love, contentment and even bliss less so, and that too is Sahasrara. In today's fractured world, finding moments like these has become more and more important. To find this 'bliss', we need to silence the chatter (*vrittis*) in our minds; we need to cultivate an internal quiet. This does not come easily.

The crown chakra is associated with the following psychological and behavioural characteristics:

* Consciousness

* Awareness of higher consciousness, knowledge of what is sacred

* Connection with the formless, the limitless

* Realisation

113

* Liberation from limiting patterns

* Communion with higher states of consciousness: ecstasy and bliss

* Presence

Keeping it in balance is therefore essential for our well-being, spiritual and otherwise. For some, this chakra is the gateway to the cosmic self or the divine self, to universal consciousness. It's linked to the infinite, the universal. For others, it is a state of pure happiness and contentment. For some, Sahasrara has been lost; for others it has always been here, all we need to do is search for it.

A balanced seventh chakra allows us access to the upmost clarity and enlightened wisdom. Its energy is able to generate a blissful union with all that exists. This is regarded as spiritual ecstasy. However, an imbalance in this chakra can manifest itself as a feeling of disconnection to the spirit, a cynical attitude to what is sacred, a disconnection from the body, from earthly matters and an attitude of closed-mindedness.

Help is at hand to restore this chakra to balance through meditation (see page 116) and yoga (see pages 124-141). But a very effective alternative exists in the form of *pranayama* (alternate nostril breathing). This breathing practice balances and activates the Ida and Pingala *nadis* (see page 102):

1   Sit in a comfortable position, either on a chair or on the floor, perhaps in your favoured position for meditation.

2   Place your left hand on your left thigh or knee and move your right hand up towards your face. Rest your index and middle fingers at the third eye.

3   Place your thumb on your right nostril and inhale through the left nostril. Hold your breath for 2-3 seconds. Now close the left nostril with your last two fingers and release and exhale from the right nostril. Again, inhale from the right, close the right nostril with the thumb and then exhale from the left. Repeat the procedure 5-7 times on each side.

The yantra and associated deities

The yantra for the seventh chakra is unlike any of the others. In Sanskrit, the name *sahasrara*, means 'thousandfold', and the lotus used here is said to have a thousand petals. The petals, arranged in 20 layers with 50 petals in each, come in all the colours of the rainbow. In some versions, the lotus appears to be bell-shaped, almost hat-like; in others, it is depicted simply as a circle. The lotus has been a potent emblem in India for more than two thousand years. The plant grows in muddy water and bursts into bloom when it rises to the surface, symbolising human growth and the nurturing of our spiritual selves as we rise towards the sun.

The bija (seed) mantra

For some, the seventh chakra has no mantra, and is best opened through silent meditation. For others, like the sixth chakra, Ajna, the seventh is associated with the mantra om (see pages 43-44). This is said to help cultivate a connection with the spirit and the whole universe or higher power. It can also help to reduce over-attachment to material things and the physical world. Some believe it stimulates the pituitary gland in the brain.

There are four parts to the seed mantra om. They are: 'ahh', 'ooo' and 'mmm' and the silence that follows. 'Ahh' represents the start of the universe. As you vibrate with it, you could feel it above your stomach. 'Ooo' represents the energy of the universe and you will feel its vibrations in your chest. 'Mmm' represents transformation. As you vibrate the sound, you should feel it in your brain. The last sound, when the long 'mmm' has ceased, takes us into the deep silence of the Infinite, the Void itself, that of Infinite Consciousness.

Meditations

1   Sit in a comfortable place for meditation. Take a long and deep breath. As you exhale, move your attention to the top of your head and imagine a violet chakra. The dark violet glow of the chakra illuminates your mind and your body.

2 Imagine a big, white lotus with its petals closed in the same place as your crown chakra. Look at the lotus and contemplate its shape, colour and texture.

3 As you pay attention, the lotus slowly starts to swirl along with the chakra.

4 One by one the petals of the lotus start to open. As the first layer flowers, you see un-countable rows of more petals still to open.

5 With every new petal opening the lotus starts spinning faster. You realise that every such opening leads to yet another layer of closed petals. The blooming of the lotus is a process of infinite stages.

6 Now see your seventh chakra spinning with equal strength. The chakra's violet light washes over you and fills every cell, every pore of your body.

7 Breathe deeply and feel the energy from your crown chakra connecting you to the sky above and to the earth below, and to everything in between, so you become one with existence.

8 Rest in this awareness.

9 When you are ready, blink your eyes open and stand up ready for the rest of your day.

* * *

1   If you can, find a quiet place outside, in the garden, on the
    roof, somewhere private. In the evening or the night would be
    preferable. Take a candle or a torch of some kind to help you find
    your way. If you cannot, then indoors will be fine too.

2   Sit down in a comfortable position for meditation. Place your
    right hand over your heart, and let fingertips of your left hand
    graze the ground beside you. Close your eyes. Settle into your seat,
    feeling the solidity of the ground beneath you, the support of your
    connection to the earth. Out of that support, allow your spine to
    rise, the crown of your head to soar into the heavens.

3   Connect to the flow of your breath. Feel the sacred quality of that
    connection - this process of inhale and exhale that is with you for
    the duration of this body's time here.

4   Sensing each rise and fall - each coming and going - in its fullness,
    ask yourself, 'Where does this breath come from?'

5   Is it possible for you to consider that, as you breathe in and out,
    a force beyond you is providing the very breath to you which
    sustains your life? It is within you and all around you. It is the
    stuff of everything, and beyond this body and this life. Can you be
    open to such a possibility?

6 If you can, allow yourself to name this force in your life: Spirit, Mother, God, Love... Contemplate this presence... What might it look like to you, feel like to you? When do you feel most connected to the sacred?

7 When you are ready, bring your attention back to your breath. Exist in your breathing. Then, gently blink your eyes open, move your fingers, arms and legs, and stand up. After a moment or two, you can get up and carry on with your evening.

Part Three

CARING FOR YOUR CHAKRAS

Moving into balance

Caring for yourself, for your body, for your spirit, for your mental and physical health, starts with awareness. Awareness of your lifestyle, the things you eat and drink, how much you exercise, your ethics and morals, and so on. It is important that we choose how we want to live our lives. Of course, no one chooses to suffer ill health, but life does inflict wear-and-tear on both body and mind, whatever lifestyle we choose.

As we have seen, chakras have been a part of people's lives for over 2,000 years and, if you have read this far, you have now joined that group. By now you will have developed an awareness of the seven major chakras, and by meditating on them, as described in the chapters on the individual chakras, you will have been able to open them up and begin to develop an awareness of how they feel, how they might affect you, and whether they are balanced or not. In this section, we are going to look more closely on how to develop a regular care regime for them and how to heal or realign them if they become unbalanced or blocked.

We have already examined the benefits of meditation in your regular chakra care, and it is a good idea to start any session on chakras with a few moments of meditation, perhaps combined with some appropriate mantra chants. In terms of healing, yoga poses, which are often known by the Sanskrit word *asanas*, are by far the most effective method. The chakras have been linked with the practice of yoga since the 10th century BCE, a connection that is still holding strong. This is thought to be because the practice of bending, stretching and twisting *asanas* helps our energy and life-force (*prana*) flow through our bodies.

Undertaken regularly, yoga is likely to keep your chakras well balanced. For this purpose, they are best done in order (starting at the bottom and moving up the spine) one after the other. However, if you should develop a blockage, the healing *asanas* that follow have been chosen with each specific chakra in mind to help you target any one for particular attention.

Note

Yoga should be taken seriously. Done incorrectly or inappropriately, it can result in injury. The best way to practice it is to join a reputable school or join a class run by an accredited yoga teacher. If you are pregnant, recovering from an operation, suffer from back pain, high blood pressure, heart problems, unsteady blood pressure or sugar levels, or are recovering from a hip, knee or back fracture, you should not be attempting to practice these poses.

If you feel any pain when practising any of them, please stop immediately. Never push your body beyond its natural limits in any pose. If in doubt, please go to your doctor for advice.

Balance the chakras with yoga

You need to do a little preparation for a yoga session. Much of this will be the same as for a meditation session, but it is helpful to remind yourself of these things before you start so that you are not interrupted or disturbed. Find a quiet and preferably uncluttered room in your home for yoga practice. Dress in comfortable clothes, in which you can move easily. Tracksuit bottoms, leggings and a T-shirt are ideal. Yoga is always practiced in bare feet. It is essential that you have a yoga mat.

You may have demands on your time that dictate when you can do yoga, but with the rays of the early morning sun coming through the window would be ideal. Open the window to let in some fresh air if appropriate. Plan to do your session before a meal rather than afterwards, make sure you listen to the call of nature before you start. Drink a little water, if you are thirsty. You are now ready to warm-up.

Start with a simple breathing practice. The exercise below is designed to encourage even, steady breaths.

BREATH AWARENESS

1   Sit on a chair, placing your feet on the ground, hip-width apart, with your knees directly above. If your feet don't reach the floor, use books or blocks to support them. Alternatively, sit on the floor

cross-legged if you are comfortable doing so, using a firm cushion to sit on so that your back does not collapse. You can also place supports under your knees if they are uncomfortable.

2 For either seated position, gently press the sitting bones down and lengthen the spine so it is upright but not rigid. Relax the shoulders down away from the ears. Rest your hands on your lap. Gently close your eyes if you are comfortable doing so; otherwise half-close them and cast your gaze softly downwards.

3 Mentally scan your body from the head downwards, noticing any areas where you are holding tension - the facial muscles, the shoulders, the abdominal area. Equally notice areas that feel open and relaxed, not tense. Notice all the different sensations of the body.

4 Now bring your awareness to your breath. Without trying to change it, start to observe the quality of the breath - the texture, the rhythm, the speed. Is the inbreath shorter or longer than the outbreath? Notice all the varying sensations of the breath as it flows in and out of your body.

5 Watch each breath for its duration, observing with acceptance (rather than frustration if it doesn't meet your expectations).

6 After a few minutes, start to follow your outbreath from its start to its end. Notice whether you allow it to run all the way to the

end, or whether you curtail it and start breathing in before you have fully breathed out. If this is the case, see if you can allow the outbreath to reach its natural conclusion.

7 Be patient and don't worry if it's not possible. It is a process. The most important thing is for the breath to be natural and not forced.

8 Notice how the navel moves towards the spine towards the end of the outbreath, and how there is a natural pause at the end of the outbreath if you allow it to take place.

9 Notice how the next inbreath arises out of this pause and how the inhalation will deepen naturally as a result of the fuller outbreath.

10 Follow the breath for a few minutes and when you are ready to end the practice, slowly bring your awareness back and start to gently move the arms, legs, fingers and toes before standing up.

After the breathing exercise, give yourself a few moments to gather your thoughts. When you are ready, the following *asana* will help you engage the chakras in preparation for the particular healing pose or poses you wish to practice. If you are a complete beginner or unsteady on your feet, then you can try it sitting in a chair. Use a chair that offers firm support. If you are going to use a chair, you must ensure that your feet are firmly on the ground, hip-width apart, and your knees are in line with your ankles.

TADASANA (MOUNTAIN POSE)

1 Stand with your feet hip-width apart. Ensure your feet are in line with each other.

2 Root down with the heels and the balls of your feet, spread and extend your toes, draw up the foot arches.

3 Draw your knees and thigh muscles upwards.

4 Press the top of the inner thighs back and the tailbone forward. Draw the lower abdomen and navel in and up.

5 Lengthen the spine upwards, lift the breastbone, allowing the shoulders to relax back and down; broaden the chest.

6 Lift the crown of the head up while pressing the soles of the feet down, particularly the heels and the mounds of the toes, into the ground.

7 Extend your arms down the sides of the body, palms facing your thighs. Gaze straight ahead and breathe steadily. Remain in the pose for 20 seconds.

Root chakra healing pose

Vrksasana (Tree pose)

1   Stand in Tadasana (see page 127).

2   Put your weight on your left foot; raise your right leg and bend it
    at the knee. Place your raised foot on the inner thigh or the inner
    shin of your left leg. (Avoid placing the foot on the inner knee.)
    Your toes should be pointing downwards.

3   Join your palms together at the heart (as in prayer position).

4   If you feel unstable, place a hand on the wall for support.

5   Let your spine lengthen upwards as you press the foot of your
    standing leg firmly down.

6   Feel the sense of being grounded as you root down.

7   Gaze straight ahead at eye level. This will help you to balance.

8   Stay as long as feels comfortable and then return to Tadasana.

9   Repeat on the other side.

'Like a tree you have to find your roots, and then you can bend in the wind'
Angela Farmer

Sacral chakra healing pose

Utkata Konasana (Goddess pose)

1   Stand in Tadasana (see page 127).

2   Step your feet wide apart (about 3-4 feet, depending on your
    height). Turn your toes slightly out.

3   Start to bend your knees, extending them in the same direction
    as your toes. Make sure your knees are correctly aligned and not
    collapsing inwards.

4   Lower your hips down to the height of your knees, if possible,
    but only go as far as feels comfortable. Take the tailbone slightly
    forwards and lengthen the spine upwards, keeping the torso as
    upright as possible.

5   Press down evenly on the soles of the feet.

6   Extend your arms out to the sides at shoulder height. Bend your
    arms at the elbows so that your palms face forwards, the fingers
    upwards, to form a right angle.

7   If you have a shoulder injury, rest your hands on your thighs.

8   Stay in the pose for 20-30 seconds, or as long as feels comfortable,
    then press through the feet in order to come up. Then bring the feet
    back together.

Naval chakra healing pose

Virabhadrasana (Warrior I pose)

1 Stand in Tadasana (see page 127).

2 Turn to the side of mat, extend your feet approximately 3-4 feet apart.

3 Raise your arms above your head, palms facing each other. Yours arms should be straight and shoulder-width apart. (If your shoulders are tight or uncomfortable, take your arms wider apart.)

4 Turn your right foot 90 degrees to the right, turn your back foot in to the right.

5 Bend your right knee. Your right knee should be positioned over your right heel, not collapsing inwards and not going beyond the heel.

6 Press down on your left outer heel; press your inner left thigh back; take your tailbone forwards. Stretch your body upwards. Gaze straight ahead.

7 Hold for 15-20 seconds, then come up out of the pose. Repeat on other side.

Heart chakra healing pose

Bhujangasana (Cobra pose)

1 Lie prone (front-side down) on the floor.

2 Stretch your legs back and press the front of your thighs and feet into the ground. Draw your tailbone to the ground.

3 Place your hands flat on the floor by the sides of your chest with your elbows hugging the sides of your body.

4 On an inhalation, start to lift your chest off the ground by pressing your hands firmly down and starting to straighten the arms.

5 Draw the navel up towards the chest, drop the shoulders down away from the ears, lift the sternum without the front ribs flaring.

6 Ensure the backbend is evenly distributed throughout the spine to avoid putting pressure on the lower back.

7 Do not strain the back by trying to come up too high. Keeping the elbows bent rather than straightening the arms completely will help avoid any potential strain.

8 Stay in the pose for up to 30 seconds, then, on an exhalation, lower your body down and rest.

Throat chakra healing pose

Setu Bandha Sarvangasana (Bridge pose)

1 Lie supine (on your back) on the ground, and bend your knees and place your feet firmly on the ground with your heels directly under your knees; your feet should be parallel and hip-width apart.

2 Extend your arms by the side of your body, palms face-down. Press the arms into the ground.

3 Press down with your feet to lift your hips slowly off the ground using your arms for support. Extend your tailbone towards the knees to lengthen your lower back; then lift a little more (never forcing) and move your chest in the direction of your chin.

4 Check that your thighs remain parallel, lifting your outer hips up and releasing your inner thighs down towards the floor.

5 Remain in this position for approximately 30 seconds, or as long as feels comfortable, and then slowly come down.

Third eye chakra healing pose

Balasana
(Child's pose)

1 Kneel down on all fours.

2 Your knees should be slightly more than hip-width apart. Bring
   your big toes together. Move your sitting bones back to rest on
   your heels. You can place a rolled-up blanket or towel under your
   feet if there is discomfort in the front of the feet, and/or, similarly,
   between the backs of your thighs and your calves if your sitting
   bones don't reach your heels.

3 On an exhalation, bend forward from the hips, keeping the front
   of your body long, and rest your torso between your thighs.

4 Place your forehead on the ground, or, if it does not reach the
   ground, rest your forehead on a block (or book). Your head should
   not hang without support. Observe the place where your forehead
   meets the ground or support.

5 Extend your arms out in front of you, palms face-down.

6 This is a resting pose – there should be no discomfort in your knees,
   legs, shoulders or back. Let your breath be easy and fluid.

7 Rest in this position for up to 2 minutes.

8 Exit the pose on an inhalation, pressing your hands into the floor
   to lift up your body.

Crown chakra healing pose

Savasana
(Corpse pose)

This is an excellent exercise to rebalance the crown chakra, but it can also be used to finish any chakra healing session.

1 Sit on the floor, extend your legs out in front of you and slowly lower yourself to the ground until you are lying supine.

2 Let your arms and legs fall away from the sides of your body. Turn your palms to face the ceiling, let your legs and feet relax out to the sides. Ensure your limbs are as symmetrical as possible to enable optimal relaxation.

3 Place a pillow under your knees if there is any tension in your back or, alternatively, you can support the lower legs on the seat of a chair.

4 Place a folded blanket under your head and neck if your head is tilted backwards.

5 Close your eyes and allow your body to relax; surrender the weight of the body to the ground beneath you.

6 Keep your attention on your breathing, and try to remain completely still.

7 Stay in the pose for up to 5 minutes, then slowly bring your awareness back, open your eyes, draw your knees up and over to the right and then push yourself up to a seated position.

Feeding the Chakras

Keeping your energy points in balance is helped by a healthy diet. The best diets are based around a little meat – if you are a carnivore – plus vegetables, grains and fruits. We are all encouraged to 'eat the rainbow' and this is a philosophy based on Ayurveda, the 'science of life', a system used in India for thousands of years to bring the body into a healthy and vitalised state of balance. Food of certain colours encourages healing within your body. Choosing foods of those colours that are in

tune with the colours of the chakras, the cycles of the seasons, and the time of the day will help develop a calm and nourished body. Spend a bit of time choosing the freshest meat, vegetables and fruit you can.

MULADHARA

The root chakra is represented by the colour red, for energy. If you are feeling run-down, fatigued, burnt-out, lazy or lethargic, red foods such as tomatoes, strawberries, raspberries, radishes, pumpkin and beetroot will help to

boost your energy levels and your body temperature. Also choose root vegetables, such as carrots, potatoes and parsnips, as well as onions and garlic. Protein-rich foods, like eggs, meat, beans, tofu, soy products and peanut butter will also bring benefits. Cook with spices like paprika and pepper.

SVADHISTHANA

The sacral chakra, also known as the creativity chakra, is located at the navel and associated with the colour orange. It governs your confidence and self-worth, so if you are low on these and feel unworthy of love then eat sweet fruits like mangoes, melons and oranges. Vegetables such as carrots, sweet potatoes and butternut squash will also help you regain control and balance in your life. Honey and nuts are also recommended. For cooking, use spices like cinnamon and vanilla to add flavour.

MANIPURA

This is called the solar plexus chakra, affects your ego and self-esteem, and is represented by the colour yellow. Yellow food is a natural mood enhancer, so if you are sad or depressed, eat fruit

like pineapple or bananas, or vegetables such as corn on the cob or yellow peppers. Dairy products, like milk, cheese and yoghurt are also helpful, as are grains such as rice, cereals, flax and sunflower seeds. Robust spices, such as ginger, mint, turmeric and cumin will flavour your cooking, along with more subtle flavours from camomile and fennel.

ANAHATA

The heart chakra, associated with matters of love, of course, is also affected by stress, fatigue and acidity. Its colour is green and the healing process can be helped by eating leafy vegetables, such as spinach, broccoli, cauliflower, cabbage and kale. You could even put them in the juicer for a healthy breakfast drink. Either that or serve up a big salad with the tastiest leaves you can find, adding some avocado and grapes along with basil, thyme and coriander. Green tea during the day can also help in rejuvenating a steady emotional frame of mind.

VISHUDDHA

This chakra is associated with the throat, and represents our power and responsibility through the way we communicate. If this chakra is blocked we might have difficulty in expressing ourselves, perhaps because of a cold, a sore throat or an ear infection. It is associated with the colours blue and black, and a healthy bowl of blueberries or blackberries is sure to hit the spot. Tree fruits, such as apples, pears, peaches and plums, are also helpful. To soothe a sore throat, drink water, fruit juice and herbal tea.

AJNA

The third eye, as it is popularly known, is located in the centre of the brow of your head, just above the eyebrows. It is the seat of wisdom, intuition and perspective and can  therefore be vulnerable to frustration and anger when out of balance. Feed it with foods that are calming such as chocolate, maybe washed down with a little red wine. This chakra's colour is indigo so try cooking some purple foods, such as aubergines, make a salad with radicchio, or go for a simple plate of fresh grapes, plums and figs. You can also boost the flavours of your cooking with allspice, cardamom or sage.

SAHASRARA

The highest form of chakra, called the crown chakra, represents your higher self and opens up your communication with the universe. In general, this chakra does not need feeding, instead benefitting from fasting or detoxifying, which can help in awakening spiritual communication. In addition, burning incense such as copal, frankincense and juniper can help cleanse the air around you and nourish the chakra as you meditate.

Healing the Chakras

Yoga, meditation and a selective diet are not the only options open to those wanting to maintain the health and balance of their energy centres. The use of essential oils, energy healing techniques, gems and crystals are also widespread, particularly when it comes to healing. This might be by: clearing unwanted energy, like stress, from the system; dissolving blockages, such as pain or tension; increasing the flow of vitality through the body; or even increasing one particular type of positive energy when you need it, like calm or optimism. But do they really work?

Essential oils

Essential oils are aromatic compounds found in the leaves, flowers, roots, stems, bark and seeds of plants. They have been in use since the age of Ancient Egypt, for therapeutic, cosmetic and ceremonial purposes, offering the promise of improvement of both mood and health. In plants, the oils serve various functions: assisting pollination, repelling pests and predators, fighting disease and encouraging cell regeneration. For humans, their use is effective in the short and long term, as an aid to physical wellness, supporting massage, yoga and meditation, clearing chakras of unwanted energy, and maintaining emotional balance among other things.

There is scientific proof of this. Essential oils are antibacterial, antiviral, antifungal, antioxidant, sedative, analgesic, antispasmodic, cleansing and antimicrobial. Because of their tiny molecular size, and because they are fat-soluble, essential oils can penetrate cell membranes and can therefore pass from the blood into the brain fluid in the central nervous system. Oils can disrupt viruses and repair damaged cell replication. They can clean receptor sites leading to improved cell communication, re-programme DNA, and deliver oxygen to tissues. They are also used to treat bacteria, such as MRSA, blood clots, stress and disease-causing free radicals. They are known to calm moods, help with relaxation, and improve sleep. It is estimated that 25 per cent of commercially available medicines contain plant derivatives. They are used in a number of commercially available products, such as personal-care items, household cleaners, aromatherapy candles and mosquito repellents.

Essential oils enter the body through the nose, skin and mouth, from where they will reach the bloodstream. These multiple methods make oils easy to use for adults and children. Perhaps the most common use is through the nose. Many people use a diffuser to scent a room creating a range of atmospheres, though they are also useful to inhibit airborne bacteria and help those with breathing difficulties. For an instant hit, you can simply put a drop of oil in the palm of your hand, rub both hands together, and breathe it in deeply. Because oils can be calming, soothing and energising, and because they have easy access to the brain, this is a fast and easy way to affect mood. Essential oils are often diffused in clinics and hospitals because of their calming properties.

Because of their molecular make-up, these oils penetrate the skin quickly, having an instant, localised effect. This kind of application is good for occasional pain, muscle aches, headaches, acne, bruising, burns, rashes and as insect repellent.

These oils can be very strong and are often diluted with a 'carrier' or 'base' oil, such as coconut or almond oil. It is important that you read the labels on any essential oil products to understand the recommended dilution for your purpose. It is particularly important that you do this if you have sensitive skin or are using the oils with children or infants (see note below). They are also a wonderful aid for massage, particularly chakra massage. It is believed that our thoughts and actions are absorbed through each chakra. When negative energy flows through a chakra it begins to spin too fast or too slow, making it unbalanced. This can affect us physically, emotionally and spiritually. Massage, reflection, meditation and energy work using essential oils can help restore balance to each of the chakras. There are a number of essential oils that resonate with each chakra. Here is a recommended starter list:

Muladhara (the root chakra)
CEDARWOOD
MYRRH
PATCHOULI

Svadhisthana
(the sacral chakra)
JASMINE
ROSE
YLANG YLANG

Manipura
(the solar plexus chakra)
BLACK PEPPER
CARDAMOM
SAGE

Anahata (the heart chakra)
NEROLI
PINE
ROSEWOOD

Vishuddha (the throat chakra)
CHAMOMILE
FRANKINCENSE
LAVENDER

Ajna (the third eye chakra)
SANDALWOOD
LEMON
ROSEMARY

Sahasrara (the crown chakra)
LIME
MANDARIN ORANGE
FRANKINCENSE

Though it is much rarer, some oils can be ingested. For example, peppermint oil has been found to be effective in combatting the effects of Irritable Bowel Syndrome (IBS). However, a number of essential oils are not only extremely strong, they are also toxic. It is also true to say that, like medicines, they can affect people in different ways. So, the advice is **do not ingest essential oils** unless you do so under the advice and guidance of a trained herbalist.

Essential oils have their critics, of course. They can be expensive because of the labour-intensive work involved in producing them. They are wasteful, for example, it takes 13.5 kilos of lavender flowers to make a 15ml bottle of essential oil. They have potential side effects, which could be serious for babies and pets, and they are unregulated. Please consider the following warning before you consider using them:

Important to note

Essential oils are very strong. If you are pregnant or are intending to use them on children under 12, it is recommended that you visit your doctor to ask for advice.

If you have sensitive skin and are using an oil for the first time, you should do a skin sensitivity test first. Put a few drops of diluted oil on your inner thigh and wait 24 hours to see if any irritation or redness occurs.

Avoid application on sensitive areas, like the eyes, genitals, inner ears and anywhere you have broken skin. The best places for application are the bottom of the feet, the wrists and the back of the neck. Massage after application increases the blood flow and maximises oil absorption.

Energy healing

Energy healing is any therapy that uses the energy of the human body to bring the body back into balance so that it can begin to heal itself. Given that these techniques use the body's life-force (*prana* in Hindu practices, *qi* in Chinese medicine), they are closely associated with the chakra energy centres. There are a number of different schools of thought in this area, but those most relevant to the study of the chakras are reiki, reflexology, acupuncture, colour and sound therapy.

Reiki is a Japanese practice that was developed by Dr Mikao Usui in the early years of the 20th century. A Reiki healer uses the palm of their hands, without touching the patient, and uses their own body as a channel to direct universal energy into the patient. During a session, the healer's hands are placed in the auric field (see page 24) over the location of all seven major chakras, usually starting with the crown chakra. Healers are taught not to direct the energy, just to let it flow where it is needed. Reflexology works on the basis that there are pressure points in the feet and the palms of the hands that relate to different parts of the body, and that working with these pressure points can help to ease problems in the associated bodily areas. For maintaining chakra balance, the most important of these is an area right the way along the arch of the foot, which controls our spinal reflexes. Thirty seconds of massage on each foot should restore the balance.

Acupuncture originated in China and has become a popular form of alternative healing around the world. The practice involves fine needles being inserted into the skin at various defined points around the body in order to balance the flow of *qi*. Western doctors tend to view the practice as a way to increase blood flow by stimulating the nerves, muscles and connective tissue in various parts of the body rather than proper medicine. But research has shown that acupuncture is helpful in the treatment of headaches, hypertension, depression, back pain, nausea, rheumatoid arthritis and other conditions.

Colour is simply light of varying wavelengths and frequencies. Electromagnetic waves constantly surround us, and colour is part of those waves. Every single cell in the body needs light energy. Our cells absorb colour, and this affects us on every level: physically, emotionally and spiritually. It is thought that the colours of the rainbow: red, yellow, green, blue, orange, violet and indigo resonate with the chakras, the body's main energy centres. Colour therapy is the practice of visualising the relevant colour, along with repeated exposure to that colour, wearing clothes of that colour and eating foods of that colour (see page 142) in order to speed up healing processes.

Sound healing, also known as vibrational healing, is believed to date back to Ancient Greece. The basic principle behind it is that the entire universe is in a state of vibration. This includes every organ, cell, bone, tissue and liquid of the human body, and the electromagnetic fields that surround it. If we are not resonating with some part of ourselves or our surroundings, we become dissonant and therefore unhealthy, our naturally healthy frequency becomes a frequency that vibrates without harmony, creating illness. Sound healing might involve listening to music or other sounds, singing, dancing, meditation or playing an instrument in order to restore the harmonic vibrations we need to restore our physical and emotional well-being.

Good vibrations

The ancient Egyptians believed that gemstones had the power to restore health and often buried deceased family members with them tucked into the layers of linen cloth in which their bodies were wrapped. Since then they have gone in and out of fashion, not as a healing aid for your ailments, but rather as a method of soothing the soul. Today, they are undergoing something of a resurgence in popularity. Some claim this is because in today's fast-paced world more people are turning to old traditions to relieve the stresses of everyday life. Others see gemstones and crystals as a natural antidote to the energy-suck of technology that we deal with at work and at home. However, there are also those who claim we have a sympathetic resonance with crystals, and researchers are said to have been able to detect electrical energy emanating from quartz crystals when they are placed close to a chakra. The stones must be cleansed in water and then put outside in the sunlight or moonlight which will energise them.

The basic idea is that crystals carry certain energies that can have a positive effect on our own. In a similar way to magnets, crystals and gemstones use energy to attract or repel. When you place certain stones over certain parts of your body, they interact with your individual chakras. Your energy transforms, vibrates, pulses, moves and shifts in accordance with the properties and energetic signature of the particular crystal.

As you will have read in the chapters on the individual chakras, each is associated with a number of gems and stones. These are listed as follows:

Muladhara (the root chakra)
RUBY
BLOODSTONE
GARNET

Anahata (the heart chakra)
JADE
PERIDOT
ROSE QUARTZ

Svadhisthana
(the sacral chakra)
CARNELIAN
FIRE OPAL
TOPAZ

Vishuddha (the throat chakra)
BLUE TOPAZ
AQUAMARINE
LAPIS LAZULI

Manipura
(the solar plexus chakra)
TOPAZ
YELLOW TOURMALINE
EMERALD

Ajna (the third eye chakra)
DIAMOND
EMERALD
SAPPHIRE

Sahasrara (the crown chakra)
SAPPHIRE
AMETHYST
CELESTITE

If you were to visit a 'healing crystal' practitioner, they would most likely get you to lie down and relax before placing appropriate stones near the chakra points. This is said to realign, rebalance and reenergise the chakras back into their appropriate functions. Some suggest that you place crystals in your home or hold them in your hands while meditating or, indeed, carry them with you throughout the day.

For some, crystals have been successful in preventing headaches, relieving stress, improving mood, even bringing peace and happiness. But scientists have been unable to prove claims that they work as medicine. If you believe in them, they might make you feel better through the perception of 'good vibrations' and that perception may help alleviate some emotional or spiritual stress.

Index

Acknowledgements

Firstly, I would like to thank Vanessa Daubney and Tania O'Donnell at Arcturus Publishing for commissioning the book and seeing it through to publication. Thanks to Dani Leigh for the beautiful design. Special thanks too must go to Charlie Hartley, a yoga teacher from Kent certified with the British Wheel of Yoga, whose help, advice, suggestions and detailed instructions on how to achieve the best healing poses were generously given and immensely helpful (www.yogahartley.co.uk). I am also indebted to the following:

Books: the classic work on chakras in the modern age, *Wheels of Life* by Anodea Judith (Llewellyn Publications, Woodbury, Minnesota, 1987/2016), is the best place to start. Also useful in more practical ways was *The Chakra Bible* by Patricia Mercier (Stirling, New York, 2007).

Websites: Wikipedia, in particular the citations which invariably provide you with a comprehensive bibliography on the subject at hand, is always a great place to begin your research. The following websites were also either useful or inspirational or both, providing ideas and explanations: bodywindow.com, brettlarkin.com, britannica.com, chopra.com, gaia.com, hareesh.org, mindbodygreen.com, newworldencyclopedia.org, spiritualresearchfoundation.org, timesofindia.com, wanderlust.com, yogapedia.com

Picture Credits

C.W Leadbeater images on pages 29, 30, 38, 50, 62, 74, 86, 98 and 110 are courtesy of the Mary Evans Picture Library. All other images are courtesy of Shutterstock.